Duke East Asia Nexus

Volume 4 Issue 1

2013

This past summer was the most harrowing in my short tenure as the Editor-in-Chief of DEAN. It seemed like we had only just said goodbye to our seniors when the bad news hit us: four more of our fine editors would not be coming back for the coming semester (all of them flung across the far corners of the globe, being 'go-getters' and whatnot). Yet we've somehow managed pull ourselves back from the brink and survive it all. So I thought I'd begin this little aside with an informal DEAN retrospective, to remind all who hold this book of the journey it has taken from that bygone era of the mid 2000s:

DEAN began in 2007 as a student organization centered around an interest in East Asia. In '09 we began publishing the first peer reviewed journal that dealt exclusively with issues concerning Asia. Taking our cue from the journal Foreign Affairs, the DEAN prime-directive focused our attention squarely on student academia in the political, historical and sociological sciences. Yet these categories could hardly hope to capture the diversity that is 'East Asia'. So we set our selves the task to cast our nets wider and spread the web of our nexus, and I'm proud to say that the Duke community responded with the amazing series of work contained within these pages. I hope that in this issue we have distilled the essence of what is so quintessentially DEAN while reinvigorating the organization as a whole. This issue marks the culmination of a project begun under my predecessors Hannah Yi and Paul Horak, to whom more is owed than can be said through words alone. Special thanks must be reserved of course for our faculty advisor Simon Partner, and of course the daring Leo Ching who have together helped steer our fledgling organization these past few years.

I hope you will take the time to peruse these pages for our more unique pieces, some choice works include the gripping historical-narrative penned from the insights Emily Feng gained from interviews with Tiananmen survivors and the spell-binding story set in revolutionary China written by Ian Zhang, to the prolific Rachel Leng's exploration the subaltern-narrative complex within Dream of Ding Village in what will sadly be one of her last pieces published with us. Of course each and every piece in this bound pack of paper and ink is the result of the hard work of our amazing writers and the dedication of our amazing editors, and it is to them that the greatest thanks goes to.

I am honored, proud, and humbled to be able to present to you, the reader, the Duke East Asia Nexus Vol. 4 Issue 1.

Tenzing Thabkhe Thondup

EDITOR-IN-CHIEF
DEAN PUBLICATIONS
FALL 2013

The Duke East Asia Nexus publication is chartered by the Duke Student Government and is a member of the Undergraduate Publications Board. It receives funding from the Asian Pacific Studies Institute, the Department of Asian & Middle Eastern Studies, and the John Spencer Bassett Memorial Fund.

We publish all accepted work that relates to East Asia biannually through this print journal, and continuously on-line.

VOLUME 4 ISSUE 1 2013

{CONTENTS}

FEATURES & ESSAYS

ON THE ROAD: ARTS, LITERATURE & REVIEWS

Ethnic Identities in China:
a History and a Comparison

The idea of race, while hotly debated and contested in the United States, carries enormously different connotations in the People's Republic of China. This paper seeks to provide a brief background to the existence of informal Chinese racial groups, as well as the formal groups established as a result of the 1953 national census. Through an examination of historical background to concepts of race in ancient China, as well as methods used by the PRC in establishing the current 56 ethnic groups in China, the paper identifies and discusses the imperfect relationship between racial groups and genetic similarity among the dominant Han group. A comparative analysis of race in America and race in China ensues, concluding that while the two nations differ in their evaluation on the political and social dimensions of race, both nations' perceptions of race are invariably linked to factors such as length of settlement, common history, political motivation for the introduction of racial groups, and linguistic similarity.

Haoxiaohan Helen Cai *is a public policy major at Duke University pursuing minors in history and political science. She served as the Duke East Asia Nexus president in 2013, and was a co-founder and director of the Duke UNC-China Leadership Summit.*

In ethical and medical arenas today, the idea of race in society is ceaselessly contested, defended, deconstructed, and redefined. In America, the term race and all its implications carry a sharp, two-edged sword: race is seen both as a pawn of oppression and as a means of recognizing human differences in an increasingly scientific world. The American understanding of race is mired in historical inequalities with present socio-political consequences and individualized for each person. It is self-prescribed, which simultaneously complicates the applicability of race in pharmacogenetics and frees the individual in terms of self-expression. No matter in which country the race-debate is waged, the discussion is fierce. However, what must be noted is that race means different things in different countries.

This paper takes to the exploration of group identities within nations in which the focus is on the interaction and history of majority groups with minority groups, regardless of whether the majority group considers itself a race or an ethnicity. Both the terms of ethnicity and race are popularly confused within the American paradigm of identity, and this paper does not attempt to provide an exhaustive definition. Instead, it studies how group dynamics have come to exist within the bounds of a country's chronology.

An exploration of race and identity in another great nation, the People's Republic of China (PRC), reveals how beliefs about nationality, ethnicity, and identity are molded both through centuries of coexistence and comparatively sudden centralized policy. Factors such as historical belief, physiological difference, government policy, and geographic population distribution all affect the way a national identity is conceived. Currently, nation which compose one-fifth of the total world population houses 56 ethnic groups that the government officially recognizes. Of those, 91.5% are in the majority Han group. The other 55 groups are considered ethnic minorities. The groups were brought together in the landmass known as the PRC by thousands of years of tribal conquests but were only recently codified into clearly delineated groups when the Chinese Communist Party took power in 1949.

Han Chinese: A History

In understanding how the Han ethnic group became the world's largest ethnicity, ancient Chinese history and folklore must be examined. The Han historian Sima Qian (司馬遷: 145BC – 82BC) attributed the Han name to the legendary Yellow Emperor (Huangdi黃帝), who was thought to have battled against his brother, the Flame Warrior (Yandi炎帝), for the right to rule the people from 2698-2597 BC. After his victory, the Yellow Emperor reigned in a region named Han Zhong, and subsequently his subjects adopted the initial part of his name for their own and became the Han people as his nation flourished and expanded geographically. Originally, the descendants of the Yellow Emperor lived around the Yellow River, China's second longest after the Yangtze, which runs a circuitous course from the Pacific Ocean into China's northern half.

Centuries after the rule of the Yellow Emperor, the first Chinese dynasty mentioned in Chinese records emerged under the direction of the Xia. It was quickly overpowered by the Shang dynasty, which was eventually absorbed by the Zhou dynasty. During the Zhou, Han culture was spread outward through conquests, and also pulled further into the south of China. Ruling for four hundred years (206BC – 220AD), the Han dynasty solidified its grasp Chinese history by ruling for four hundred years (206BC – 220AD). It expanded the borders of imperial China to the Hexi Corridor in Gansu, the Tarim Basin in Xinjiang, modern north Vietnam, North Korea, and Southern Mongolia. With each conquest, the emperors would begin a series of reforms of Sinicization, which entailed the linguistic and cultural adaptations necessary for the conquered people to assimilate into Han Chinese life. The language taught was Hanyu: Han language, and its writing system, Hanzi, Han characters.

Subsequent to this Sinicization were periods dominated by the non-Han dynasties. Through careful preservation of the status quo, minority groups from the fringes of ancient China (the Mongols in the thirteenth century, the Manchus in the seventeenth) came to rule the Han majority. By carefully absorbing the Han culture and not abolishing previously-existing institutions of identification, the outside-rulers preserved much of the Han status quo and in turn received a calmer transition. Regardless of dynasty, the people under Chinese rule have historically clung to the Han Chinese identity. Chinese scholars in premodern times attributed this gravitation

towards the Han group as evidence of the Han group's cultural and technological superiority. After all, inventions by the Han include gun powder, seismological detectors, canal locks, paper currency, cartography, pendulums, the compass, the civil service examination and much more. However, recent studies, such as that of David Wu, have found this claim to be "at best, a myth":

> The Chinese people and the Chinese culture have been constantly amalgamating, restructuring, reinventing, and reinterpreting themselves; the seemingly static Chinese culture has been in a continuous process of assigning important new meanings about being Chinese. (Wu 162)

Instead of being the irresistible superior culture once imagined, the new populations seemed to join into the culture due to pragmatic reasons: for access to goods and a chance at social mobility.

Formal Shifts in Chinese Identification (Influence of the West)

In the three hundred years rule of the Manchus under the Qing dynasty, a great amount of changes in identity occurred at a startling pace. The Qing era experienced a huge population growth that made resources scarce. In response, family ties required strengthening in order to "control market towns [due to] the gradual erosion of social order and organizational disorders caused by demography pressures" (Dikotter 14). As such, families increased their reliance on the cult of patrilineal descent, and more credibility and unity arose out of individual jiazu (family tribes). Simultaneous to the lay awareness of family lineages was the stricter classification of 'race' in the court. Manchu leaders, aware and growing fearful of total assimilation into Han culture, started drawing distinct boundaries around the four major 'races' in the courts: "Han, Manchu, Mongol, or Tibetan" (Crossley).

The earliest consolidated effort to study Chinese race from within came in 1898 during the Hundred Days of Reform. After over two hundred fifty years of Manchu rule under the Qing Dynasty, a faction of reform-minded civil examination candidates demanded for overwhelming national changes in governance. Kang Youwei, one of the candidates who feared further exploitation under Western imperialistic powers, approached the Emperor Guangxu with 40 edicts that would modernize the Chinese imperial rule. One of the edicts called for an examination on the effects of race in China. Historian Frank Dikotter writes:

It was the product of a fusion between different indigenous strains of knowledge and foreign discursive repertoires, with the principal object of political attention being the species. The scientific category of 'race' and the administrative category of 'population' were heralded as objects worthy of systematic investigation. (Dikotter 12)

Although all the edicts ultimately were revoked by the Dowager Empress Cixi following her coup d'état, the reasons behind the reforms were clear: China was becoming more and more influenced by Western ideas. Chinese people thought in terms of race, calling themselves the Yellow Race, after the royal color of the Yellow Emperor, and ceaselessly comparing themselves with the White Race in attempt to escape the fate of the conquered Black and Red Races (Dikotter 13).

The Formal Formation of the *Minzu*: 1954

Concrete steps towards constructing a national identity followed immediately behind the birth of the People's Republic of China. The new Communist government (CCP) possessed an inchoate recognition of the ethnic groups within China, and certainly did not expect to receive over 400 responses to the fill-in question for race the 1953 census (Aird). The large number of professed races may have arisen as a result of government-promised benefits to minority groups: a seat for every ethnicity on the National People's Congress, promised limited autonomy for ethnic minorities, and national recognition of identity (Mackerras). Regardless the motivation for the 400 groups, the CCP now had to determine once and for all how many of the claimed ethnicities it could grant formal recognition.

On May 15, 1954, the government dispatched the Yunnan Ethnic Classification Team to taxonomically determine the number of ethnicities in Yunnan province, which singly had yielded 260 of the 400 different responses. The team worked with a tight 6-months deadline, and heavily relied on pre-existing linguistic research to delineate ethnicities. The Yunnan researchers believed that there was a strong correlation between language and ethnicity. Linguistics was considered to be a reliable means of approximating linearity, because it "lent itself readily to the formulation of reductive, hierarchical phylogenies" and "enabled the taxonomist to establish the existence of a common ancestry between seemingly disparate groups without relying on the subjective claims thereof" (Mullaney 12). Factors such

Haoxiaohan
Helen Cai

as dress, culture, and geographic distribution were also taken into account. The Yunnan team, along with several other groups around the country, provided reports that gave the Party the 56 ethnic groups in place today.

Government Benefits to Minorities

Current national benefits afforded to minorities are many. Minority members are excluded from the One-Child policy implemented in the 1970s, and are allowed to have more than one child. Minority children have access to several large state-operated scholarships, and are given a certain advantage on their college-entrance exam scores. In government posts, affirmative action for minorities is a well-established practice. Most importantly, some minority groups with religious and political differences are granted ethnic autonomous areas (Xinjiang, Tibet, etc.) (Sautman). In recent years, parents of newborns were able to choose to use either the father or the mother's ethnicity for the newborn's hukou (household registry), which has since resulted in an increase of reported minority births due to the desire to claim minority benefits (Wang 88).

Economic Inequalities
Between the Han Majority & the Minorities

Despite these apparent advantages, however, the de facto reality of minority life is harsh. Even with the execution of affirmative action, minorities lag behind the Han majority in employment, education, and quality of life. A large part of this discrepancy can be attributed to the unequal playing field. Many minority groups exist outside of large urban areas, and tend to suffer from inferior educational institutions, which, in China's competitive, high-education seeking job field, damages the vocational pursuits of minority children. The preservation of minority languages in ethnic schools is a mixed blessing: cultural heritage is passed down, but limits the amount of education on Hanyu, which is critical in most capacities. The typically rural nature of minority group concentrations also limits the kinds of employment available.

Social Inequalities
Between the Han Majority & the Minorities

Historically a nation of conquest and assimilation, China today is still highly polarized on the issue of ethnicity. Affirmative action programs have reaffirmed sentiments of Han superiority and

Han largesse among the majority, and it is evident from cultural stereotypes that the nation is still a long way from complete ethnic equality. Misunderstandings and folktales about people of different ethnicities are still commonly tucked into pockets of the country. "To this day, for instance, the Cantonese describe the Tanka, a population group of boat-dwellers in South China, as people with six toes on each foot: they are claimed to be of non-Han descent. The small toenails of the Mongols are said by the Han to be cloven, while minorities in Hainan have long been alleged to have a tail" (Dikotter 93).

Two major views contend about the nature of the current majority-minority balance. Dr. Gladney at UChicago holds the more cynical view of the dynamic and frames it in terms of oppression: "Minority is to the majority as female is to male, as 'Third' World is to 'First,' and as subjectivized is to objectified identity". Dr. Wu of MIT expresses a more long-range and hopeful view of Chinese ethnicities and believes the lack of permanence and definition of the Chinese identity leaves much room for reconciliation: "since most Chinese have believed that the Han people were the race of China, one that had absorbed people of all languages, customs, and racial and ethnic origins; the meaning of being Chinese in the sense of ethnicity, culture, citizenship, or residence were almost never addressed" (Wu 162). Whichever is the more accurate description, the strong identity of the Han majority, with its thousands of years of history, is here to stay, and the minority must adapt itself to that understanding.

Genetic Analysis of Ethnic Group Variation

What is interesting about the Chinese concept of ethnicity is that it is simultaneously lineage-based and incredibly reliant on cultural and linguistic factors. In present society, the Han majority seems to be united in its cultural heritage, but a genetic analysis provides interesting results about the unity of the group. In 1997, Cavalli-Sforza, Ruofu Du, and Chunjie Xiao published a paper describing the genetic distances between Chinese populations. The three used gene frequencies based on 38 loci to calculate the genetic distances between Han subpopulations and ethnic minority groups, with the hypothesis that genetic differences can be explained by natural geographic barriers. In China's case, the natural barrier used was the Yangtze River, which scissors China into two halves: a northern and a southern region. The team discovered that:

Haoxiaohan
Helen Cai

... the mean genetic distance between northern Han subpopulations and northern ethnic minorities (244.7) is close to that among the northern ethnic minority (289.9), the genetic distance between southern Han subpopulations and southern ethnic minorities (304.1) is also similar to that among the southern minorities (250.0), but the mean genetic distance between southern and northern Han subpopulations (517.0) and that between southern and northern ethnic minorities (598. 9) are much greater, nearly double. (Cavali-Sforza et al. 617)

The team drew the conclusion that in both north and south China, the Han regularly intermixed with local ethnic populations, which subsequently caused their genetic structures to converge in likeness. These genetic distances also indicate that the Han subpopulations on either side of the Yangtze have more in common with their neighboring ethnic populations than their Yellow brothers across the river. However, despite such an interesting study, genetics will have little impact on social group identification and Han majority identity. As Manning Nash observes in his 1962 paper, "Race and the Ideology of Race", society may ignore or incorporate scientific information about race and identity as it pleases.

Comparisons Between Ethnic Identity in China & Racial Identity in America

A parallel assessment of the roots of national, ethnic, and racial identity between the history-rich Chinese and the newly-amalgamated American underlines acute differences and also striking similarities. Main differences include the sudden coalescing of people groups in America versus the gradual assimilation in the East. In China, where physiological variation between the groups are nuanced, China has found the need to involve the government in defining groups. In America, where physical features are more prominent, race is self-identified. In both countries, group identity is couched in majority terms. Both identities of people groups are largely resistant to scientific challenges to their permanence. These characteristics say much about the adaptability of group identity, and its ability to transcend country borders.

The origins of the Chinese and Americans are vastly incomparable. While the Chinese were forced to live under different ruling 'races' due to the dynastic cycle, Americans were almost uniformly dominated by people of European descent. Although the Han people were ultimately in possession of most of China's imperial dynasties, sporadic punctures in the tapestry of Han rule steadied and familiarized the populace with different rulers. This history of multiethnic governance may have attributed to early Han and ethnic admixture, whereas white supremacy in the United States propagated centuries of anti-miscegenation laws.

Americans were faced with a stark palette of peoples immediately distinguishable from one another, while the Chinese were differentiated more by nuanced characteristics like language and customs. Of those peoples, China is more uniform, with a 92% Han majority; America is more diverse with a 73% white majority. Colonists, slaves, and immigrants shared no common history, whereas the history of the Yellow Emperor extended several centuries back in the Chinese consciousness. Black, white, and Indian Americans were instantaneously forced to adopt a social hierarchy, whereas China's social hierarchy was based on civil service tests.

Identification of ethnicity and race are also determined differently: Chinese ethnicity is determined by lineage from parents and approved through the government, and American race is self-reported and self-identified. The two governments also hold drastically different views on the usefulness and purpose of group distinctions. In China, the motivation behind creating the 1954 ethnic groups was both political and social. China wanted to encourage ethnic diversity as a political aspiration and symbol and to target disadvantaged areas with more aid. America requires the reporting of race mostly for socio-economic information and to right historic wrongs. Unsurprisingly, both governments tried to allocate benefits accordingly: China is able to offer many exceptions and aid to its minority and proudly displays its support of minorities, whereas America is more subdued in its allocation of minority resources.

Some aspects of group identity are universal. Given a history of oral and cultural tradition, group identifications are unlikely to be buffeted by scientific discoveries that run counter to widely-held perception. As the Cavalli-Sforza report indicated, group identity can easily superceed or absorb true lineage In both China and the United States, scientists did try to either fortify or negate the existence of race and ethnicity. Dikotter's critique of Chinese scientists who blundered through race analyses could be equally applied to comtemporary racial scientists in America:

Haoxiaohan
Helen Cai

A variety of cultural intermediaries – social reformers, professional writers, medical researchers, university professors – scientized these folk notions of common stock and legitimized racial discourse through appeals to the authority of science (Dikotter 19.)

The failure of the 'scientific' findings to sway common perception of race or ethnicity owes much to the crux of group identity history that operated very well without scientific assertion or refutation. The tendency for a dominant group to overshadow or succeed over a minority group is also apparent both in China and in America. Although affirmative action operates in both countries, institutionalized inequalities (in home locations, in educational opportunities, in unconscious stereotypes) are still running rampant.

In conclusion, attributes like length of settlement, composition of peoples, common history of groups, political motivation behind race and ethnicity identification, and linguistic similarity play a big role in group identity formation. Group dynamics formed in different nations will inevitably be divergent and unique, since each people have a unique history and unique experience living in a region. China's case demonstrates that ethnicity can sometimes be used a political tool to right inequalities and unify a diverse nation. Chinese ethnicities are used to distinguish between peoples that have coexisted in the same area for thousands of years, and simultaneously seek to rectify current injustices.

Works Cited

Cavalli-Sforza, L. L., Chunjie Xiao, and Roufu Du. "Genetic Distances between Chinese Populations Based on 38 Loci." *Science in China* 40.6 (1997): 613-21. Print.

Crossley, Pamela. 'The Qianlong retrospect on the Chinese-martial (hanjun) banners'. Late

Imperial China, no. 1 (June 1989), pp. 63-107

Dikötter, Frank. *The Construction of Racial Identities in China and Japan: Historical and Contemporary Perspectives.* Honolulu: University of Hawai'i, 1997. Print.

Gladney, Dru. "Representing Nationality in China: Refiguring Majority/ Minority Identities." *Journal of Asian Studies* 53.1 (1994): 92-123. Print.

Hannum, Emily, and Yu Xue. "Ethnic Stratification in Northwest China: Occupational Differences between Han Chinese and National Minorities in Xinjiang." *Demography* 35.5 (1998): 323-33. Print.

Mullaney, T. S. "Ethnic Classification Writ Large: The 1954 Yunnan Province Ethnic Classification Project and Its Foundations in Republican-Era Taxonomic Thought." *China Information* 18.2 (2004): 207-41. Print.

Wang, Fei-Ling. "Organizing Through Division and Exclusion: China's Hukou System - Fei-Ling Wang." Stanford University Press, 2005. Web. <http://www.sup.org/book.cgi?id=7081>.

Wu, David YH. "The Construction of Chinese and Non-Chinese Identities." *Daedalus* 120.2 (1991): 159-79. Print.

Haoxiaohan
Helen Cai

China's 1935 Currency Reform: a Nascent Success Cut Short

This paper argues that the Nationalist Government had little alternative to the radical 1935 Chinese Currency Reform in view of its lack of coherent financial system during first part of the 20th century. The success of the project can be found in the economic data from 1936, and from the effective institutions which started to develop from the reform. This growth, however, was cut short by the military spending sequestered to fight off the Japanese invasion in 1937. The currency, still weak from factors such as international politics and a poorly organized banking system, failed to absorb this expansion and fell into a state of hyperinflation. Without a credible currency, the post-war recovery by the Guomindang (GMD) was impotent, and actually helped to lay the groundwork for the Communist rise to power. This paper shows that although the currency reform was executed successfully, the economy was not able to stabilize before the disruption and destruction of the Japanese invasion, and that the resulting hyperinflation helped precipitate the demise of the Nationalist government on the mainland.

Noah Elbot *was raised in Beverly, MA before joining Brown where he studied Economics and East Asian Studies. Noah has worked in a diverse set of fields, from serving as a legislative intern on international policy and speech writing for then-Senator John Kerry to working on public partnerships with the Providence Public School system. Noah received a scholarship after freshman year from Brown's East Asian Studies department to work as an ecological field assistant at a research base in the jungles of southern Yunnan Province and later attended LSE's Entrepreneurship Summer School in Beijing. In the fall of 2012, Noah studied at the Chinese University of Hong Kong and is preparing to return for a master's program as part of the Brown Plus One partnership. In Providence, Noah is also a leader with the Brown Meditation Community, climbs and whitewater kayaks, and is a proud uncle to his 3 year-old nephew, Oliver.*

The success or failure of the Nationalist experiment during the short-lived Chinese Republic remains a contentious topic among historians. Economically, the newly reunited nation was still suffering from the Warlord Period, the first Sino-Japanese War, and a multitude of internal rifts. The Nationalist government, headed by Chiang Kai-shek, took a range of measures in an attempt to stabilize the country. Central to this period is the 1935 currency reform, which removed China from the silver standard and pegged it to a mix of foreign currencies. This paper argues that the currency reform was a necessary move, allowing China a coherent financial system that had great potential for growth. The Japanese invasion in 1937, however, was systemically destructive, disrupting the fundamental market structure and throwing the financial institutions into disarray. This paper aims to show that, although the 1935 currency reform had potential for development and economic stability, the underlying institutions were fundamentally shaken by the Japanese invasion and unable to weather the subsequent reconstruction. The resulting hyperinflation factored strongly into the defeat of the Nationalist government on the mainland during the Chinese Civil War.

~China at the Beginning of the Republican Period~

In 1928, when the Guomindang (GMD) began its rule from Nanjing, China could hardly be called unified. The Warlord Period had left much of the country's organizational infrastructure and markets in tatters, and foreign investment was negligible.[1] During the Warlord Period and even before, each territory had developed its own local currency, ranging from paper to silver or copper. Exchange rates were mostly based on local custom, or approximation to the tael system, which was roughly 40 grams of silver.[2] Dr. Wen Pei Wei, in his influential 1914 work *The Currency Problem in China*, states that "of a currency system it can be seen that China currently has none... No one single unit of currency in the Chinese system, if it can be called that, serves the function [of standard of value] for the country

[1] Yuru, Wang. "Economic Development in China (1920-1936)." in *The Chinese Economy in the Early Twentieth Century*. Ed. Tim Wright. New York: St. Martin's Press, 1992. p.74.
[2] Very roughly. In practice, the tael measurement differed from city to city even from product to product;, the measurement of payment would be different. See "The Currency Problem in China" by Wen Pin Wei

as a whole."[3] Though many historians refer to this period's currency as conforming to a silver standard, this is misleading, because there was no coherent system of convertibility among the currencies. Currencies were subjectively pegged based on quality, weight, and other criteria. Growth rates were low during the era in spite of steps taken by the Nationalists to increase foreign trade and rapidly build infrastructure, such as railways.[4] In addition to hindering enterprise, it was almost impossible to effectively tax the diverse range of currencies. The Nationalist government struggled to provide small fixes and unified exchange systems; however, it became obvious that a large-scale reform was needed in order to modernize the financial system.

The problems caused by the chaotic system came to a head in 1934. China had been shielded from the original market crash in 1929; however during the 1930s, the Great Depression caused a precipitous drop in foreign trade and investment as countries turned to isolationist, protectionist policies.[5] Post-imperialist China was increasingly dependent on foreign investment for both imports and exports, and the lowered purchasing power of trading nations was devastating to local economies.[6] By some estimates, foreign investment made up 20% of overall investment in China during that period.[7] The primary cause of the collapse, however, was not a drop in consumption but rather the rise in silver prices in rest of the world.[8] As the value of the gold standard currencies of the world powers dropped with the global market crash, the price of silver rose significantly, lessening China's trade advantage. The rising silver price also set off an even more insidious trend: the steady flow of silver out of China. Because silver was not an official currency of China, the metal itself was subject to the global market price set in the London trade houses and therefore went to the highest bidder.[9] This caused silver to flow from rural areas into urban areas – pooling primarily in Shanghai's international exchange markets – before jumping offshore.[10] By 1934, more than half of the specie

[3] Wen Pin Wei. "The Currency Problem in China" *Columbia Studies in the Social Sciences*. Ed. Yalman, Ahmet. New York: Columbia University Press, 1914. p. 311
[4] Yuru, Wang. "Economic Development in China (1920-1936)." p 66
5 Shiroyama, Tomoko. *China During the Great Depression: Market, State and the World Economy 1929-1937*. Cambridge: Harvard University Asia Center, 2008. p. 10
6 Ibid. p. 92
7 Dernberger, Robert. "The role of the Foreigner in China's Economic Development." *China's Modern Economy in Historical Perspective*. Ed. Perkins, Dwight. Stanford: Stanford University Press, 1975. p 30
8 Shiroyama. p. 6
9 Ibid. p. 35
10 Ibid. p.103

that remained in the country was in Shanghai.[11] As silver left China, prices varied wildly and a fall in agricultural output and other sectors of the economy followed.

The crisis was further augmented by the policy decisions of the United States. By 1934, President Franklin Roosevelt had practically removed the US from the gold standard in response to the Great Depression. This move, however, was balanced by increasing dependence on silver and minting silver dollars. The United States' new appetite for silver birthed to the Silver Purchase Act of 1934, causing global silver prices to skyrocket with the new demand.[12] The precious metal was rapidly exported from Asia, causing nominal prices to fall, real prices to inflate, and subsequently the cost of living rapidly became out of reach for most of the population as the supply of currency dwindled. As silver prices fluctuated, banks began to rely on the values of commodities, especially real estate, in order to finance loans both in Shanghai and the rural markets. Compounding the issue, the Japanese government released the Amou Doctrine in 1934, stating that Japan would oppose any foreign assistance to China.[13] Laying claim to the China as a Japanese suzerainty, this Asian Monroe Doctrine left the Nationalist government without a clear chance of receiving foreign assistance. In June 1935, the shock was too much for the Chinese markets to handle, and the real estate market subsequently collapsed.[14]

The 1935 Currency Reform

In view of the market instability, it became clear that silver could no longer be relied upon as a stable value holder for the Nationalist Government. In order to ensure the economic well being of the country, the decision was made to find a new currency peg. The 1935 Currency Reform remains controversial as to how efficacious it was in stabilizing domestic markets. The next section will give a brief outline of the proceedings surrounding the reform and the nature of the changes themselves, before discussing perspectives on the success of the project.

Due to the Amou Doctrine, Great Britain and the US were wary of the political consequences of defying the Japanese and providing

[11] Ci Hongfei. "On the Consequences of the 1935 Currency Reform." *The Chinese Economy in the Early Twentieth Century.* Ed. Tim Wright. New York: St. Martin's Press, 1992. p.194.

[12] Shiroyama, p.155

[13] Ibid. p.170

[14] Ibid. p.166

overt assistance to the Nationalist government. England still held a policy of appeasement during the period, and US diplomacy was locked in debate over isolationism. In addition, suspicion that the Nationalist government was planning a systematic currency reform would have sent the markets spinning even further out of control. Due to these considerations, Kong Xiangxi, China's finance minister, had to conduct planning meetings in secret. Kong ended up using the US's thirst for silver to China's advantage, trading for about $100 million USD, which was used as a stable reserve base to launch reform. [15] From November 1935 to December 1936, banks issued new paper currency, which was completely detached from the silver standard. Chinese were required by mandate to hand in their current silver reserves in return for the new currency, mostly in order to supply the silver promised to the United States. The Government and the newly formed central bank were careful to do a controlled release of about Ch$2 billion* worth of the new notes in order to prevent inflation, and precautions were taken to distribute notes gradually and fairly.[16] In the few months following the release of the notes, the government waited to see whether the Chinese would trust the new, unified currency.

The stabilizing core of the new currency was its peg to combined exchange rates of Great Britain, the United States, and Japan. In order to promote confidence, the currency, called the *fabi*, was fully exchangeable into any of these global currencies, addressing the primary issue with the old silver coinage. Kong and the central bank decided to keep secret exactly how the *fabi* was valued between the three currencies.[17] This was both the biggest strength and weakness of the *fabi*. The decision to peg the new currency to all three currencies was a clever diplomatic maneuver: Chinese took no sides in the growing tension among the world powers, no nation held complete control over the value of China's currency, and in the competition to become the world's reserve currency, each of the pegged countries began courting China to link solely to their money. The valuation was used as a bargaining chip to try to secure both loans from the British and more advantageous silver trade terms with the Americans.[18] In addition, the fully convertible currency allowed for easier global trade, and greater government control over import-

---

[15] Ibid. p.192

* Note: Ci Hongei defines Ch$ as the fabi in 1935. See "On the Consequences of the 1935 Currency Reform." p. 206 for more information

[16] Ci Hongfei, p.199

[17] Shiroyama, p.188-190

[18] Ibid.

export imbalances. As the new currency began to diffuse throughout the market, it seemed that domestic confidence began to grow.

One argument against the currency reform was that the convertibility made the new currency inherently inflationary, and was therefore not sufficiently stable to encourage private enterprise and investment. Carl Riskin of Columbia University argues that Chinese industry had a considerable surplus during the 1930s, which was subsequently mismanaged by a culture naïve about private investment. He notes that often, workers would donate their salaries to political groups or government projects instead of investing it themselves in private enterprise. Riskin claims this cultural peculiarity was encouraged by the government, and remained during Communist rule up until the reform period almost 50 years later.[19] Other historians, such as Robert Dernberger of Stanford University, take the position that the Nationalist government had a more direct role to play in the inflationary effects. Dernberger posits that the Nationalists left the silver standard in order to use the currency as their own personal bankroll, printing money to offset deficits. According to Dernberger, this inflationary spiral prevented the Nationalists from competing with Japanese growth.[20]

A third position, taken by Phillip Richardson of the University of Bristol, is that the Nationalist government had, in fact, followed the Japanese model too closely. By removing the silver peg, Richardson argues that the centralization of power gave the Nationalists the ability to run state supported enterprises similar to in Japan. This system led to a vindictive form of bureaucratic capitalism, whereby government officials were spending public money for private gain. He also notes the disproportionate amount of government spending focused on the GMD military, Chiang Kai-shek's personal project. [21]The distrust of private enterprise led to low private investment, preventing the government from meeting its full potential. However, in contrast with other historians, Richardson does admit that much of the economic hardship of the Republic was situational rather than due to mismanagement. He discusses efforts by the GMD to promote import substitution strategies, which were fatally limited by China's relatively small market share in global markets and price-

[19] Riskin, Carl. "Surplus and Stagnation in Modern China." *China's Modern Economy in Historical Perspective.* Ed. Perkins, Dwight. Stanford: Stanford University Press, 1975. p 51
[20] Dernberger, p.47
[21] Richardson, Phillip. *Economic Change in China, c. 1800-1950.* Cambridge, UK: Cambridge University Press, 1999. p 97

taker status.[22] According to Richardson, most of the obstacles the GMD encountered were endemic to the state of post-imperial China, rather than the fault of the Nationalists.

Critically, some of these economic assessments are founded upon a flawed direct comparison between China and the growth of Japan in the early 20th century. Dernberger fails to take into account institutional, societal, and geographical differences between the two nations, as well as the varied impact of the Great Depression. Some accounts also overly emphasize the success of the Communists post-1949 as a position by which to criticize the growth of the Republic in the 1930s.[23] Not only do these figures seem inflated in comparison (and are possibly even incorrect)[24], but they fail to take into account the effects of the Great Depression and the tense state of the world on the brink of World War II.

The primary argument against a negative assessment of the 1935 currency reform is the data from 1936 up until the beginning of the Japanese invasion. Bond prices began to rise through the middle of 1936 and into 1937, giving the government more capital to finance debt incurred from the recovery process. These measures were paired with limitations on fiscal spending in a concerted effort to balance the budget. Consequently, Prices "re-inflated" to the level they were at before the run on silver, though this rehabilitation was slow to filter down into the rural retail market.[25] The economy quickly regained traction in international markets as well, as foreign investment rose and the trade imbalance began to right itself. Within the year, the Republic's credit rating reached new levels, garnering international loans from the US and Great Britain for infrastructure improvements.[26] In March 1937, the Governor of the Central Bank of China, T.V. Song (also Chiang Kai-shek's brother-in-law) announced, "There is no gainsaying the fact that during the past eighteen months the whole outlook in the country, politically, financially and commercially, has changed completely and for the better."[27] In the period of less than two years, there was an economic optimism in China that had little precedent in modern times.

The essential strength of the fabi was its easy convertability to foreign currencies, especially those of the three pegged world powers. Although this policy instilled confidence in a populace that

[22] Ibid. p.96-98
[23] Riskin, p.49
[24] Ci Hongfei, p.75
[25] Shiroyama, p.195
[26] Ibid. p.196
[27] Ibid. p.197

had never known a floating paper currency, it also severely limited the actions of the Nationalists. The government could not simply print money to finance its debt lest it face high inflation due to the so-called impossible trinity of monetary policy. The very stability of the system relied on the government's frugality.[28] This runs contrary to Richardson's argument that state enterprises were too powerful. In fact, they made up for less than 10% of productive capital in 1936. The rest was domestic industry and, to an even larger degree, foreign investment.[29]

There were remained key flaws in the Chinese system. The rural banks still relied mostly on collateral loans, and credit was not forthcoming outside of the major cities. The Nationalists were unable to finance many of the infrastructure projects needed to truly industrialize the country and were spending too much money on military development. However, these remaining problems were small compared to the progress gained within just 18 months. The stability of the new currency, combined with an especially successful harvest, seemed to signal a new, optimistic era for the Chinese Republic.[30]

War With Japan

The only nation that stood to lose from China's rise was Japan. Removal from the silver standard brought down the prices of Chinese exports, which now competed for market share in South East Asia.[31] A fiercely nationalistic Japan was also incensed by US and Great Britain's defiance of the Amou Doctrine by funding loans into China in support of the Nationalist government. Economically, Japan took a heavy-handed approach extracting raw materials and resources from China.[32] The Japanese military also expanded its presence in Manchuria, a contested northern region of China. Aside from the economic competition, there was also a powerful element of racial and cultural animosity.[33] Hopes for a peaceful Asian conclusion quickly faded as both nations prepared for war. On July 7, 1937, the so-called Marco Polo Bridge incident sparked a full-out invasion by Japan.[34]

---

[28] Ibid. p.199
[29] Ci Hongfei, p.202
[30] Shiroyama, p.198
[31] Ibid. p.196
[32] Ci Hongfei, p.202
[33] Spence, Jonathan. *The Search for Modern China.* New York: W.W. Norton & Company, 1990. p. 444
[34] Ibid. p.445

The progress of the war moved quite swiftly, and by 1938, the country was fragmented into many smaller regions controlled by the Japanese, GMD, or CCP forces to one degree or another.[35] The GMD was pushed out of Nanjing and the entire Yangzi river delta, retreating back to the traditional southern stronghold of Chongqing. The war brought with it many atrocities by the invading forces, the most conspicuous of which being the Rape of Nanjing. The highly developed eastern region of China was under Japanese occupation until the end of the war in 1945 and suffered immensely during this period.

The *fabi*, at least at the beginning of the war, actually faired quite well. The Japanese attempted to attack the currency directly by installing their own reserve bank in the occupied region of China. They released a new currency and issued edicts stating that use of the Republic's currency would be severely punished.[36] In spite of this, the *fabi* was actually still the most secure mode of exchange, as the new Japanese currency was overprinted and prices inflated. Japanese policy was, however, successful at replacing Chinese enterprises with industries imported from Japan, from transportation to utilities.[37] As the war continued, so did the disruption to economic activities. The Yangzi closed in 1937, effectively halting internal trade, and as Japan took control of most major ports, the GMD were increasingly sequestered to central China. Between land and infrastructure destroyed in battles, economic assaults on both enterprise and currency, and the retreat from Nanjing, almost all of the foundation of the Republic's economy had been destroyed.

In 1939, World War II broke out in Europe. Initially, the effects of World War II were little felt by Republican China; however international aid quickly dried up, as US and British supply lines were unable to reach the GMD, which was now mostly landlocked in central China. In 1941, with the Japanese bombing of Pearl Harbor, the Pacific was no longer a travel route for foreign ships, halting aid and international trade.[38]

As the war wore on, the *fabi* finally succumbed to an inevitable end. High war spending, insufficient access to foreign support, and lack of commercial activity all led to hyperinflation. Chiang Kai-shek needed to print money in order to maintain the military forces necessary to repel the Japanese forces. From their new capital

[35] Ibid. p.451
[36] Spence, p.453
[37] Ibid.
[38] Lary, Diana. *China's Republic.* Cambridge, UK: Cambridge University Press, 2007. p. 136

Noah Elbot

in Chongqing, the Nationalists could not avoid printing excessive amounts of currency. Additionally, international aid was tepid and reserves fast drying out. Between 1938 and 1941, The US continued to buy Chinese silver in exchange for $25 to $50 million dollar loans, which could only be used for non-military spending. Unfortunately, the support was too little.[39] The resulting inflation from excessive money printing rendered the *fabi* worthless.[40]

At this point, it is worth observing the dramatic shift in stability of the fabi from the confidence of 1936-'37 to the hyperinflation of the Sino-Japanese War. Many of the characteristics of the 1935 Reform that initially seemed successful became destabilizing.

Primarily, the strength of the Republican currency became its central fault: in times when high spending was necessary, the pegged currency necessarily devalued itself. During times of peace, such as 1965, this tradeoff served to moderate government spending and power, effectively exchanging flexibility for market confidence. This self-regulating process created a high potential for internal growth but, more importantly, elicited confidence from international sources who trusted that a currency pegged to their own would be unlikely to fail. However, this was a fragile balance even during times of peace. In late 1935, the government issued high interest bonds in order to pay back debts. This caused an uproar within the Shanghai business community, as their nascent enterprises were starved for investment as capital flowed towards bonds.[41] The Japanese invasion necessitated a much more aggressive Chinese fundraising strategy than one wholly just from bonds. As the GMD needed the flexibility to finance military expansion, greater amounts of money were printed. With a lack of moderation in supply, the currency was no longer viable to be exchanged for foreign currency at the rates dictated by the government.

Subsequently, the convertibility of the *fabi* also became a fatal flaw. Consumers had been convinced to adopt the new bills due to their ability to exchange into a more stable international currency. The *fabi* relied on a self-sustaining relationship between confidence and growth. As long as growth prospects were high, then people would choose to hold *fabi* as opposed to foreign currency. This cycle raised the viability and value of the Republican currency and allowed for further growth, when confidence was high. This cycle could be observed during the 1936 economic build-up. In contrast,

---

[39] Spence, p.466
[40] Shiroyama, p.237
[41] Ibid. p.209

as growth prospects declined during the war, consumers, especially international businesses, were able to quickly convert their currency and leave the high-risk Chinese market. Even more directly, Japan was able to convert industries over to their own control more easily due to the exchangeability of the *fabi*. Additionally, as the GMD became isolated in Chongqing and foreign trade shut down, the ability to exchange money into foreign currency became much less advantageous.

Kong's diplomatic maneuvering to prevent pledging monetary allegiance to only one foreign currency also proved destructive during the war. Of the three currencies used as markers, two were at war with the other one. Even more importantly, having a stronger economic and diplomatic alliance with either the US or England over Japan might have been a boon during the early days of the invasion. If, for example, China had supported the United States dollar as the reserve currency, President Roosevelt's government might have been more generous with war supplies and financial aid. During the post-reform boom, the expansion of foreign banks into China was welcomed as a sign of increasing prosperity. Chinese merchants also developed a dependency on these banks, however, and when they left the country they took at least Ch$2.5 billion dollars with them. The foreign banks likely contained more capital than the four major domestic banks combined.[42] If the war had not occurred, China's politically neutral decision could have enabled them to benefit from all the major world powers. With the war, however, the policy left the GMD diplomatically isolated, and furthermore resulted in a mass exodus of foreign currencies and investment from China.

As can be seen above, many of the initial advantages of the 1935 currency reforms became detrimental to the Republic's economic stability. An expensive war to fend off a dominant invading army would be difficult for any currency to absorb. The *fabi* had only 18 months before the Japanese invasion to build up confidence. The fact that the *fabi* fared as well as it did during the Japanese invasion and that it was still used as a market currency for the entire war speaks to its strength. Its degeneration into hyperinflation was unavoidable considering the stress upon it and the limitations of a pegged currency.

---

[42] Ci Hongfei, p.203

Aftermath and the Decline of the GMD

The end of the Sino-Japanese War was a result of the combination of an over-extension of the Japanese supply lines and the US victory on the Pacific front.[43] The Communist forces had gained significant position during the war, in contrast to the dramatic losses suffered both politically and economically by the GMD. As a result, Chiang Kai-shek and the Chinese Republic were remanded to the diplomatic children's table, barred from participating in the Yalta conference with the other Allied leaders.[44] If they wanted to be considered a legitimate nation, the GMD would have had to sort out its own domestic affairs first—a daunting task. As stated by General Wedemeyer of the US armed forces in Asia, "if peace comes suddenly, it is reasonable to expect widespread confusion and disorder. The Chinese have no plans for rehabilitation."[45]

Adding to their troubles, China soon became the stage for a proxy war of small-scale sabotage between the US and Soviet forces. Ostensibly working together, the two powers severely botched the Japanese surrender. The Soviet's, sweeping into Manchuria to offer "assistance" just a week before the war ended, began to pilfer machinery and equipment out of Chinese factories, shipping them back to Russia.[46] They also purposefully allowed many of the recovered Japanese weapons to fall into communist hands.[47] The United States forces also mishandled many aspects of the surrender, guiding the Chinese to prioritize military formalities above governance. US diplomats pushed a resistant Chiang Kai-shek to form a coalition government with the Communists. Some American diplomats and military personnel saw this as the only hope of avoiding civil war, though the policy was highly controversial. Now in a much stronger position, the CCP paid lip service to the offers, but in reality were little interested in a power-share.

China was once again in a state similar to 1928: divided, conflicted, and destitute. Each separate area held different allegiances, with the Nationalists losing ground to the Communists' recruitment efforts. For the Nationalist *fabi*, this meant that exchange prices varied wildly from city to city, sometimes by more than 500%. This led to

---

[43] Spence, p.483

[44] Ibid. p.478

[45] Ibid. p.484

[46] Lary, p.160 The Russians did not realize, however, that the instruction manuals and controls would be in Japanese, rendering most of the stolen equipment useless.

[47] Spence, p.486

rampant speculation, exacerbating the discrepancies.[48] Additionally, famine was rampant in many areas that had fallen victim to both the Japanese and GMD scorched earth tactics. In an attempt to stem the suffering and rebuild support amongst the rural peasantry, the GMD printed more money for relief efforts.[49] In 1937, before the beginning of the war, the fabi was worth $.30 cents to the dollar by 1942 , it had dropped to $.03.[50] The hyperinflation can also be observed in wholesale price indexes from the era. Taking September 1945 as a baseline, prices in Shanghai had increased eleven-fold by the following May, and then thirtyfold by February 1947.[51]

Manchuria, having been under Nationalist supervision after fourteen years of occupied rule, was a chaotic mess. Many of the residents, having adapted to Japanese rule, resented returning to the control of the Han Chinese. In addition, both the Japanese and the Russians had looted much of the area during their withdrawal. In order to bypass the inflation of the *fabi*, the Nationalists attempted to institute a unique currency to Manchuria. This currency, however, also soon degenerated into a state of hyperinflation.[52]

Little financial assistance arrived from abroad. In the aftermath of World War II most countries were focused on domestic recovery, and international trade slowed to a trickle. The markets for Chinese luxury items such as silk were especially hard hit by this trend.[53] Direct foreign investment in China was also not forthcoming, mostly due instability caused by the growing tension between the GMD and the CCP.[54] During the period directly following the war, many businesses had shut their doors due to the confusion of the transfer of power from Japan back to the GMD. What should have been a simple process turned into chaos as vengeful GMD bureaucrats tried to freeze Japanese assets, often hurting Chinese enterprises. The lack of stability was exacerbated with abuses by state police forces, which commandeered cars and looting property all in the name of martial law.[55]

The GMD began to take desperation measures to control inflation and the rise in living costs. They attempted to peg wages to price indexes, which increased the burden on businesses. When that didn't

[48] Ibid.
[49] Lary, p.137
[50] Spence, p.486
[51] Ibid. p.498
[52] Ibid. p.495
[53] Lary, pp.159-160
[54] Yuru, p.74
[55] Spence, p.486

work, the government instituted price and wage ceilings. This effort also failed, as markets revolted against the constraints.[56] The Bank of China also attempted to curb the rapid inflation, but to no avail. To make matters worse, government debt, primarily on military expenditures from the war, was at 66% of total spending.[57] Chiang Kai-shek's government was on the verge of collapse.

On August 19, 1948, the government made one final effort. As a desperate measure, The GMD attempted to reform the entire system by releasing gold-backed currency. The reform led to chaos as people rioted in an attempt to get the mere 2 billion gold *fabi* notes released. Draconian police measures were instituted, especially in Shanghai, to make sure that only the new currency could be used.[58] However, the efforts were not enough, and as the black market rapidly grew. The new currency, despite its gold guarantee, also became uselessly hyper-inflated. China had devolved into a barter economy, and the Nationalist government was rendered economically impotent until its overthrow at the hands of the Communists.

The rapid death spiral the Nationalist government underwent seemed inevitable in view of the destruction the Sino Japanese War. Economically, it was unfeasible that the juvenile *fabi* could survive the stresses of post-war China without reform. These difficulties were, however, exacerbated by a flawed transfer of power from the occupying Japanese back to the GMD. During this period, businesses closed down, capital was being looted by both the government and criminals, and confidence was at an all time low. Workers suffered the most from the price and wage instability, causing over 1,500 strikes in 1946 alone.[59] Its power base in the urban centers now gone, the Nationalist government went from the promise of prosperity in 1936 to profound destitution just a decade later.

Initially, the 1935 Currency Reform by the Nationalist government was a success. The Nationalist government released a new currency, based upon efficient convertibility into a range of foreign tender. The economic successes witnessed in 1936 hinted at the potential of the pegged system. Unfortunately, this nascent growth was cut short by the Japanese invasion in 1937. During the ensuing period of inflationary spending, those very strengths of the post-1935 currency devolved into weaknesses, and furthermore, were met with ambivalence and indecision by the international community. Though

---

[56] Ibid. p.500
[57] Ibid. p.502
[58] Spence, p.503
[59] Ibid. p.499

remaining strong in the initial stages of the war, the currency began a fatal spiral into hyperinflation. In the post-war period, mistakes by the GMD hastened the decline of the fabi, as chaos and corruption caused by the rebuilding effort brought the economy to its knees.

Looking forward, it could be argued that the failure of the currency and the subsequent radical measures to try and revive it even directly assisted the rise of the Communist party. The hyperinflation hit urban workers the hardest, elevating the appeal of the Communist movement for labor unions. Furthermore, the Communist government's own currency, the Renminbi, seems at least partly inspired by the fabi: Today's Renminbi is pegged to a secret basket of foreign currencies, mirroring the fabi system. The relationship between the fabi and the Renminbi deserves further study. At the very least, the CCP benefitted, by learning from the flaws of the GMD's currency policy. The Currency Reform of 1935 could not prevent the the chaos of the following decade, yet still played a critical role in shaping the development of modern China.

Noah Elbot

Works Cited:

Ci Hongfei. "On the Consequences of the 1935 Currency Reform." *The Chinese Economy in the Early Twentieth Century*. Ed. Tim Wright. New York: St. Martin's Press, 1992.

Dernberger, Robert. "The role of the Foreigner in China's Economic Development." *China's Modern Economy in Historical Perspective*. Ed. Perkins, Dwight. Stanford: Stanford University Press, 1975.

Lary, Diana. *China's Republic*. Cambridge, UK: Cambridge University Press, 2007.

Richardson, Phillip. *Economic Change in China, c. 1800-1950*. Cambridge, UK: Cambridge University Press, 1999.

Riskin, Carl. "Surplus and Stagnation in Modern China." *China's Modern Economy in Historical Perspective*. Ed. Perkins, Dwight. Stanford: Stanford University Press, 1975.

Shiroyama, Tomoko. *China During the Great Depression: Market, State and the World Economy 1929-1937*. Cambridge: Harvard University Asia Center, 2008.

Spence, Jonathan. *The Search for Modern China*. New York: W.W. Norton & Company, 1990.

Wen Pin Wei. "The Currency Problem in China" *Columbia Studies in the Social Sciences*. Ed. Yalman, Ahmet. New York: Columbia University Press, 1914.

Yuru, Wang. "Economic Development in China (1920-1936)." *The Chinese Economy in the Early Twentieth Century*. Ed. Tim Wright. New York: St. Martin's Press, 1992.

The Subaltern Voice in Dream of Ding Village: Speaking to the Myth of Consanguinity Through China's Blood Crisis

Yan Lianke's novel, Dream of Ding Village 《丁庄梦》 (2006), provides a fictional account of the decline of a village inflicted by AIDS, focusing on the experiences of the Ding family across three generations. The novel paints an alarming portrait of the trade-off between capitalist progress and human well-being as China acts in an increasingly globalized world. In line with this reading, this paper asks to what extent does Yan's novel mediate the subaltern voice, providing a testimony of suffering AIDS victims in central China? Moreover, can the portrayal of Ding Village's blood-selling crisis be read allegorically in relation to Rey Chow's conception of the myth of consanguinity? By making Qiang, a dead twelve year-old boy, narrate the story from a position both literally and metaphorically at the margins, this paper contends that Yan deploys a ghosted narrator as a discursive tool to enter a site of resistance through the text. Enabling the subaltern to transcend Spivak's condition of silence, all the while enunciating a counter-discourse of broader ethical and political agency. As a thematic motif, the circulation of (tainted) blood also interrogates issues of kinship, where instead of strengthening a meaningful sense of community, the act of sharing blood ironically results in the irrevocable rupture of family relations. As such, Dream of Ding Village exemplifies how Yan utilizes literary strategies to empower the subaltern with voice and agency, dispel the myth of consanguinity by appealing to broader political and ethical ideals, and prompt a reconceptualization of the meaning of solidarity and nationhood. This paper argues that Yan's ongoing acts of revisionist history, of returning to scenes of domination and suppression, reactivates attempts at speaking that other forces have sought to obliterate. In revisiting the ruin of an AIDS village, Yan makes it speak in new ways, opening up a line of communication that enters a marginal space – a site of resistance that mobilizes Chinese subaltern vocality for counter hegemonic discourse.

Rachel Leng is a native Singaporean who moved to Shanghai, China at the age of 6. Growing up on the mainland, she witnessed Chinese society transformed by rapid globalization, spurring her interest in contemporary China's shifting sociopolitical landscape and cultural change. She graduated from Duke University in May 2013 with a double distinction in Public Policy Studies and Asian and Middle Eastern Studies (concentration in Chinese), and a minor in economics. Rachel is now pursuing a masters in East Asian Studies at Harvard University, where she intends to focus on the imbrications of modern Chinese literature, society, culture, and politics.

In the early 1990s, hundreds of blood collection stations were set up in Henan Province to supply the Chinese market for plasma (Wu et al. 2004). To persuade farmers to sell their blood, local government officials promoted blood-selling as a rural development scheme that would lift villages out of poverty. "Bloodheads," the network of businessmen and government workers running plasma collection activities, practiced unhygienic collection procedures such as reusing needles and re-injecting separated red blood cells back into peasant blood-sellers to maximize profit, causing the rapid spread of HIV through infusion of pooled contaminated blood cells (Wu et al. 2004). Nevertheless, the Chinese government took great pains to cover-up the HIV epidemic, with officials denying its severity as well as harassing journalists, physicians, and other activists who sought to document the blood scandal (Kellogg 2003).

After AIDS became public in China in 1996, Yan Lianke (阎连科) followed an American medical anthropologist to a village in the AIDS epidemic zone to practice medicine. In an interview, Yan describes his experience visiting this AIDS village for the first time: upon sighting coffins for sale and countless graves, he states that the "surprise and shock on his mind cannot be expressed with words" (Zhang 2006). His words also speaks to the psychological problems and mental anguish these villagers experienced as a result of AIDs causing internal fractures within families: married couples becoming alienated, young newlyweds blaming each other for getting infected, and families no longer "harmonious" because relatives did not want to touch each other (Zhang 2006). Upon witnessing the scale of the AIDS outbreak, Yan "felt like he had to write something." And, after three years of undercover work at AIDS villages in rural Henan, this culminated in Dream of Ding Village 《丁庄梦》 (2006)

Yan Lianke's novel, *Dream of Ding Village* (hereafter referred to as "*DDV*"), provides a fictional account of the decline of a village inflicted by AIDS, focusing on the experiences of the Ding family across three generations. The book opens in the waning years of the "blood-selling boom," where so many people have died in East Henan's Ding Village that "the graves in the village cemetery were as dense as sheaves of wheat in a farmer's field" and families have stopped observing mourning rituals such as writing funeral couplets (8-9; 17). An AIDS pandemic has spread unchecked due to local "bloodheads" who used contaminated needles, intimidation, and chicanery to extort blood from villagers and resell it to government blood banks for profit. Ding Hui was Ding Village's most notorious blood merchant, and angry villagers take revenge on him for infecting them with the "fever" by poisoning his son, Ding Qiang (10). After his murder, Qiang lingers over Ding Village as an omnipresent observer and narrates *DDV* from beyond his grave, "buried behind the brick wall of the elementary school" (10). The questions I will address in this paper are: to what extent does Yan's novel mediate the subaltern voice, providing a testimony of suffering AIDS victims in central China? Moreover, can the portrayal of Ding Village's blood-selling crisis be read allegorically in relation to Rey Chow's articulation of the myth of consanguinity? This paper contends that Yan deploys *DDV*'s ghosted narrator as a discursive tool to enter a site of resistance through the text, figuratively enabling the subaltern to speak from a silenced position. As a thematic motif, the circulation of (tainted) blood also interrogates issues of kinship, where instead of strengthening a meaningful sense of community, the act of sharing blood ironically results in the irrevocable rupture of family relations.

Representing the Subaltern Voice of AIDS Villagers in China's Central Plains

In asking the question, "Can the subaltern speak?", Gayatri Chakrovorty Spivak sparked debates about the power (or lack thereof) of subordinate voices to enunciate its experience meaningfully. Spivak comes to the categorical conclusion that "the subaltern cannot speak" because "there is no space from which the subaltern can speak," raising complex questions about the ways in which first world intellectuals aspire to give "voice" to third world subalterns (1988, 308-309).[1] Are there literary strategies that authors may utilize to allow subaltern subjects to represent themselves authentically? Or do all well-meaning intellectuals inevitably reproduce simplistic misrepresentations of their own culture's subalterns? I suggest that Yan's 2006 novel, *DDV*, negotiates this tension with a literary strategy that deploys a ghosted narrator speaking from the margins of the story's diegesis. In this way, the author (Yan) and subaltern subjects (AIDS villagers) are positioned to speak from distinct but complementary perspectives in the text.

---

[1] Originally a term for subordinates in military hierarchies, the term "subaltern" here is derived from the cultural hegemony work of Antonio Gramsci, where he refers to groups who are outside the established structures of political representation, the means through which people have a voice in their society. In her essay, Spivak further suggests that the subaltern is deprived of both mimetic and political forms of representation.

When Spivak examines the validity of the Western representation of the other, she presents the subaltern Asian woman as paradigmatic of the subaltern condition and urges feminists to speak *to* rather than *for* subaltern women, so that "the postcolonial intellectual *systematically* 'unlearns' female privilege" (295). This paper contends that the rural farmers in Yan's novel similarly exemplify the subaltern condition as figures caught "between patriarchy and imperialism, subject-constitution and object-formation" that "[disappear] ... into a violent shuttling ... between tradition and modernization" (306). In writing *DDV*, Yan admits to struggling with self-censorship, where he did not write the original story he intended and "deliberately avoided many true and terrifying situations," yet still wished to convey how "the situation in the village was so desperate" (Zhang 2006; Watts 2006). Yan's conceit of having a fictional character narrate *DDV* from beyond the grave accentuates the elusive, particularized, and radically decentered subjectivity of the subaltern AIDS villagers, enabling these figures to speak meaningfully.

Contrary to Spivak's pessimistic account of the mute subaltern, Yan's novel demonstrates the possibilities for political resistance embodied in subaltern vocality. The narrator, Ding Qiang, reveals that he was "only twelve, in [his] fifth year at school, when [he] ... died from eating a poisoned tomato [he] found on the way home from school" (10). Surrounded by people "*dy[ing] like falling leaves, their light gone from this world*" after selling blood, Qiang's death is especially tragic because "[he] died not from the fever, not from AIDS, but because [his] dad had run a blood-collection station in Ding Village ten years earlier... [He] died because [his] dad was ... a blood kingpin" (9-10, italics in original). In other words, his young life was taken away in an abrupt and undue manner. As he narrates the decline of Ding Village while the villagers struggle with AIDS, he bears witness to the demolition of his own family and hometown. Towards the end of the novel, Qiang's father has moved on from selling blood to selling coffins and "running a match-making service for the dead" (298). Ironically, Qiang plays a poignant role in the death of his own father when he "*scream[s] for dear life*" begging his Grandpa, Ding Shuiyang, to "save him" from being married off posthumously (321, italics in original). Qiang screams from "inside [his] coffin" with "cries [that] shook the heavens" and "ripped holes in the sky," finally driving Shuiyang to smash the back of Hui's skull with a chestnut stick (331-2). This macabre scene underscores that Qiang, although marginalized and ghosted, can and does speak to alter the fate of his grave and his family. In this sense, the ghosted

Qiang illustrates Yan's effort to speak back to Spivak's concerns, where the fictional character's lingering presence and narration after death simultaneously acknowledges the necessary absence yet underlines the reality of that absence inherent within subaltern positionality.

With this plot development, I suggest that Yan circumvents Spivak's assertion of the silenced subaltern by elucidating bell hooks' statements identifying marginality as a "site of radical possibility" (hooks 1990, 341). In "marginality as a site of resistance," hooks claims that the silenced can speak from "that space in the margin that is a sign of deprivation, a wound, and unfulfilled longing" that becomes "a central location for the production of a counter hegemonic discourse" (1990, 341-3). Qiang's ghosted presence exists "on the edge" between life and death (hooks 1990, 341); in the novel, he was murdered at the brink of puberty and hastily buried at the edge of Ding Village in the local elementary school because "he was too young to be buried in the ancestral grave," underscoring his character's multilayered marginality. He is literally dead silent within the novel's diegesis, yet is the very voice to which we figuratively listen as the story of Ding Village unfold. In this way, Qiang's interstitial presence represents "a site one stays in, clings to even, because it nourishes one's capacity to resist ... [and] offers the possibility of radical perspectives from which to see and create, to imagine alternatives, new worlds" (hooks 1990, 341).

According to hooks, a true explanation of subaltern experience can come from the intellectual only if the latter does not assume a cultural superiority when investigating the voices of oppressed subalterns. In *DDV*, Yan allows the subaltern experience to be spoken through Qiang's perspective – a "radical perspective" that is "shaped and formed by marginality" and enters "that space in the margin that is a site of creativity and power" (hooks 1990, 342). Thus, Yan utilizes Qiang's voice in the novel to re-present rural AIDS villagers, emphasizing a position that "inhabits marginal space that is not a site of domination but a place of resistance," a discursive intervention that allows the subaltern to "[speak] from margins... [and speak] in resistance" (343). The fictional Qiang stands in for the actual subaltern subjects that Yan met during his fieldwork and seeks to represent. By making Qiang narrate the story from a position both literally and figuratively at the margins, Yan enables the subaltern to transcend Spivak's condition of silence, all the while enunciating a counter-discourse of broader ethical and political agency.

Rachel Leng

The Circulation of Tainted Blood and the Myth of Consanguinity

If we accept that the subaltern represented in Yan's novel can speak, the question then becomes: what is the subaltern speaking about? *DDV* highlights a vast array of issues concerning the transitional tensions resulting from China's rapid modernization, government exploitation, and corrupt capitalism. This paper focuses on the thematic circulation of blood within the text, analyzing it through the interpretive lens of Rey Chow's claims about the myth of consanguinity. In her introduction to *Writing Diaspora*, Chow elucidates that "a strong single political regime, an identity based on national unity, and ... the claims to ethnic oneness − sinicization − ... are as practically effective as they are illusory and manipulative" (1993, 24). She insists that these "forces of sinicization" stem from the "myth of consanguinity" − *"a myth that demands absolute submission because it is empty"* (1993, 24, italics in original). In her view, this myth inexorably results in "the surrender of agency ... in the governance of a community" (Chow 1993, 24). As a novel overtly concerned with blood, issues of consanguinal ties and "the responsibility any individual bears for belonging to a community" becomes strikingly apparent in DDV (Chow 1993, 25). The thematic circulation of blood reveals a paradoxical situation that speaks to the myth of consanguinity: blood, rather than strengthening consanguinal or marriage relations, ironically causes internal fractures within families. Although the blood-selling initiative initially strengthens affective connections to imagined communities, these bonds to fictive kin are torn apart by the end of the novel, revealing the vacuity of the myth of consanguinity.

Set in China's disillusioned heartland and centered on a rural blood-selling crisis, the circulation of blood and kinship relations are key thematic motifs threading through *DDV*. The novel's ironic critique of consanguinity is highlighted with recurring metaphors that liken blood to water; another sardonic twist is manifest when these metaphors are used to justify the blood-selling initiative as a nation-building and rural development scheme. When blood plasma resource centers were first set up in Henan, the Director of Education entreats Grandpa to "talk to the villagers and explain that selling blood is no big deal" (29). Heeding the Director's advice, Grandpa repeatedly emphasizes that "blood is like spring water" where "the body's blood is like a natural spring; the more you take, the more it flows," assuring villagers that "water never runs dry, and

[they] can never sell too much blood" (30-1). Soon, the villagers are swept up into a blood-selling frenzy that "started as a trickle" but "soon became a stream [and] before long, ... turned into a blood boom" bringing along "the fever" that "burst upon [them] like a flood" (12; 38). It is especially unnerving when blood appears to become even more commonplace than water. Blood inundates Ding Village: "pools of red and russet, patches like congealed blood" are juxtaposed against dry riverbeds and "all day long, the air was filled with the stench of fresh blood" (31-2). Even the village trees, after absorbing "so much blood" in lieu of water, have "new leaves" ominously "tinged with pink and veins of brownish-purple" (39). These descriptions counter slogans such as "Blood is Thicker than Water" that, as Chow points out, have consistently been used to strengthen a sense of "Chineseness" amongst diasporic Chinese communities (1993, 23-24). Rather than being the viscous glue symbolically fastening kinship bonds, the novel advances imagery of blood as a watery fluid instead, fundamentally diluting the potency of consanguine relations.

The emptiness of the myth of consanguinity is underscored by the Ding family's fractured kinship between Grandpa, Ding Shuiyang, and his two sons, Ding Hui and Ding Liang. Both of Grandpa's sons' involvement with blood-selling engenders major rifts in their father-son relationship: throughout the novel, they repeatedly clash over issues related to blood, where the atrocities of the blood-selling scandal and AIDS plague overwrites the value of familial blood ties. Qiang narrates that his Grandpa wanted to "ask [Hui] to apologize to everyone and then to kill himself. *Because the sooner [his] father died, the better*" (13, italics in original). It is Hui's refusal to respect Shuiyang's request for him to apologize and atone for his role in spreading AIDS through Ding Village that results in numerous father-son altercations, including Grandpa's attempted strangling and eventual murder of his own son. When Grandpa attacks Hui, Qiang narrates the conflict as something that has "no going back" and "[can't] be undone," where despite being related by "flesh" and "blood," "father and son [were] trying to kill each other, fighting to the death" (54).

Additionally, Liang, although also sick with AIDS and consequently receives more compassion from Grandpa, still incurs the wrath of the old man. When talking about his plan to infect his wife, Liang remarks that he "hope[s] ... to give [AIDS] to Tingting, so she can't get remarried after [he is] gone," to which Granpa "[recoils], too stunned to speak" (74). These shocking

plot developments produce strong antagonistic feelings, where Grandpa wishes that neither of his sons were born. Powerful negative emotions are manifest when Grandpa curses Liang for being "a miserable excuse for a son" and avowing that "his son Ding Hui deserves to die" (164; 184). The circulation of tainted blood is at the root of these fractured family relations. This disillusioned portrayal of blood ties thus illustrates Chow's argument that a sense of solidarity grounded in "submission to consanguinity" is an empty belief that inevitably causes "the surrender of agency," social alienation, and the breakdown of meaningful relations (1993, 24).

Despite irreparably estranged relationships within the Ding family, it is intriguing that the blood-selling crisis and AIDS epidemic initially strengthens the villager's affective connection to imagined communities at both the national and local level. At the national level, the villagers are led to believe that they should spare "a few drops of blood" to "help [their] country" by replenishing the government blood banks (88). Nonetheless, when they started contracting "the fever," the national government turns a blind eye to helping these AIDS villagers, failing to provide them necessary financial and medical assistance, or even enough coffins to bury their dead. At the local level, the sardonic establishment of the village elementary school, that was once also "a temple dedicated to … the Chinese god of good fortune," as "a hospice for people with the fever" creates new relationships when "the sick villagers found that life in the school was better than they had imagined" (61; 69). Specific "rules and regulations" were even set up for "all residents of the school," enhancing the sense of a distinct political and social regime for the community (152). Romance also enters the story through the love that blossoms between Ding Liang and Lingling, two AIDS victims at the school. After being abandoned by their respective spouses, they struggle through their sickness together and fall in love. However, the narrative also states that "this paradise didn't last for long," foreshadowing the inevitable fissures within the community (70). The sense of fictive kin amongst Ding villagers are exposed as woefully empty: villagers resort to stealing from each other in their dying days, two men who take charge of the school end up wrangling over who gets to get buried with the village seal in the late stages of their sickness, and Ding Liang and Lingling both die a few days after they finally complete an arduous divorce and remarriage process to marry each other.

The novel ends with the stark image of a desolate village with not "a single soul" in sight where "people and animals had been obliterated, and the plain was barren" (341). The relational ruptures illustrated in *DDV* therefore reveal how completely the Ding villagers sacrificed themselves and their whole livelihood to the myth of consanguinity, a myth that is exposed as myopic and flawed, leaving only a hollow sense of loss and tainted blood in its wake. At this juncture, I suggest that the belief in consanguinity within kinship webs traversing Ding Village is a synecdoche of Spivak's argument about the subaltern's positionality within networks of institutional authority. Without access to an authentic kinship network, where both imaginary and real blood ties are exposed as void, all the villagers are deprived of the ability to sustain a meaningful sense of community or affective relationships with others. The portrayal of people being alienated from one another because of the circulation of blood – the same symbolic act that is supposed to establish indissoluble connections between – is deeply ironic. In the novel, this dynamic may be interpreted as a metaphor for the way the subaltern is silenced by the very same institutional networks that purportedly give them voice. Along the lines of this analysis, perhaps it is only after the myth of consanguinity is overcome that the subaltern can make claim to agency and negotiate for their voices to be heard.

DDV paints an alarming portrait of the trade-off between capitalist progress and human well-being as China acts in a globalized world. As Yan reflects, "the silence is intense" but "even in absence of voices or sound Ding Village lives on; choked by death, it will not die," turning its very existence into a text of resistance (Penêda 2012). Yan has also proclaimed in several interviews that as a native writer, he felt it was his responsibility to record what happened in Henan (Penêda 2012; Zhang 2006). In addition to DDV, Yan is well-known for novels that have gained him both critical acclaim and hardship with esteemed literary awards and harsh government bans. Thus, Yan represents a member of the literary class that Vera Schwarcz has referred to as "contemporary Chinese intellectuals [who] have become fractured vessels – broken-hearted witnesses to their own and their countrymen's suffering" (1991, qtd in Chow 1993, 25). Schwarcz further elucidates that the "internal fragmentation" of these intellectuals represents "China's best hope for recovery" through "fidelity to historical memory" (1991, 107). In this view, Yan is one such author who takes up this "important and also rather bleak responsibility" to "bring to mind both the courage and cowardice of China as a whole" (Schwarcz 1991, 107); in an effort to "forge a

social reality between truth and fiction," Yan strives to liberate his writings so that they reach and speak to readers with authenticity (Penêda 2012). DDV exemplifies how Yan utilizes literary strategies to empower the subaltern with voice and agency, dispel the myth of consanguinity by appealing to broader political and ethical ideals, and prompt a reconceptualization of the meaning of solidarity and nationhood. Yan's ongoing acts of revisionist history, of returning to scenes of domination and suppression, reactivates attempts at speaking that other forces have tried to obliterate and keep from having effects. In revisiting the ruin of an AIDS village, Yan makes it speak in new ways, opening up a line of communication that enters a marginal space – a site of resistance that mobilizes Chinese subaltern vocality for counter hegemonic discourse.

Works Cited:

Chow, Rey. *Writing Diaspora: Tactics of Intervention in Contemporary Cultural Studies.* Bloomington: Indiana UP, 1993.

Kellog, Tom. "Health Officials Seek to Avoid Responsibility for the Spread of HIV/AIDS in Rural Henan." *China Rights Forum.* HRIC Human Rights in China, 23 Feb. 2003. Web. 03 Mar. 2013. <http://www.hrichina.org/crf/article/4561>.

Penêda, Vera. "The Dream of Yan." *Globaltimes.cn.* Global Times, 19 June 2012. Web. 03 Mar. 2013. <http://www.globaltimes.cn/content/715814.shtml>.

Spivak, Gayatri Chakravorty. "Can the Subaltern Speak?" In *Marxism and the Interpretation of Culture.* Ed. By Cary Nelson and Lawrence Grossberg. Urbana: University of Illinois Press, 1988. Pp. 271-313.

Vera Schwarcz. "No Solace from Lethe: History, Memory and Identity in Modern China," In *The Living Tree: The Changing Meaning of Being Chinese Today.* Cambridge, MA: American Academy of Arts and Sciences, 1991. Pp. 88-112.

Watts, Jonathan. "Censor Sees through Writer's Guile in Tale of China's Blood-selling Scandal." *The Guardian.* Guardian News and Media, 08 Oct. 2006. Web. 03 Mar. 2013. <http://www.guardian.co.uk/world/2006/oct/09/books.china>.

Wu, Zunyou, Keming Rou, and Haixia Cui. "The HIV/AIDS Epidemic in China: History, Current Strategies and Future Challenges." *AIDS Education and Prevention 16.* Supplement A (2004): 7-17. US National Library of Medicine. Web. <http://www.ncbi.nlm.nih.gov/pubmed/15262561>.

Yan, Lianke, and Cindy Carter (trans.). *Dream of Ding Village.* New York: Grove, 2011.

Zhang, Ying (张英). "The Story of AIDS Villages: Being Alive is Not Just an Instinct [艾滋病村的故事：活着不仅仅是一种本能]." *Southwest Daily.* 南方日报, 24 Mar. 2006. Web. 03 Mar. 2013. <http://health.sohu.com/20060324/n242450967.shtml>.

The Next Big Crisis?
US-China Relations & Post-Unification Security Arrangements in Korea

Political science often engages in the art of prediction, yet often such discussions result in endless debates are of little use. And yet, with all its problems, predicting the future seems possible when we narrow down the next flashpoint to the Taiwan Straits and the Korean Penninsula.

The Koreas have received a great extent of the media coverage for their nuclear programs, missile launches and joint-military exercises. As the vibrant south stands in stark contrast to its dour cousin to the north, few ask the question of what place a singular Korea might take in a post-reunification world. With the North backed by the Chinese government and the South by the Americans, it seems almost impossible to predict which way the balance will shift. Yet a long history of invasions and imperialism, the picture while murky may yet be gleaned.

With the delicate balance of the March West and the Pivot to the Pacific now in the works; caught between the power struggles of two superpowers, issues such as the Korean unification will become especially frought with concerns of security alignment and treaty agreements.

Joel Jin-Kyu Lee *graduated from Duke in May 2013 with a double major in Political Science and Asian & Middle Eastern Studies. He spent the last summer interning at the Korean Chair in the Center for Strategic & International Studies (CSIS) in Washington, DC. Spending his time conducting research on the "royal couple" Kim Jong-Un & Ri Sol-Ju, as they had just taken center stage while also pursuing interests in nuclear negotiations, power politics and international relations.*

If you ask three political scientists the same question, I'm sure that you will receive four answers. If you line up all the world's political scientists into a single line, they would likely organize themselves into different schools rather than reach a single conclusion. However, I also believe that there is one conclusion that will be supported by most, if not all political scientists, that issues of national security often take us by surprise. What will be the next surprise, after German reunification, September 11, the financial crisis, and the Arab Spring? Last December, the National Intelligence Council specifically identified two potential crises in the Asia-Pacific for the next two decades: another Taiwan Strait Crisis and reunification of the Korean peninsula.[1]

The reunification of the Korean peninsula is an important issue in that although the world's eyes are focused on North Korea's nuclear development, the real long-term threat lies not in an improbable nuclear war started by a suicidal dictator, but in the unfolding of geopolitical tensions upon reunification. The 38th parallel currently divides two Koreas, each supported by a different superpower; once this status-quo line is lifted, the policies of both the United States and China to maintain their influence in the region will collide. More specifically, if the two Koreas unify, what happens to the U.S. alliance with South Korea and Chinese support for North Korea? Will the U.S. and China clash over regional hegemony in a strategically important region located between China, Japan, Russia, and the U.S.?

The questions are all the more important in the changing context of the rise of China and the U.S. pivot to Asia. If Germany achieved reunification in the context of a supreme U.S. vis-à-vis a retreating Soviet Union, Korean reunification will occur amidst a rising power China and the standing superpower the U.S. How willing will Washington be in accommodating Beijing's power in the region, and also in adjusting the network of bilateral alliances that dates back to the Cold War? And how will China react once it perceives an opportunity to push back U.S. troops in the region, once Korean reunification eliminates the need to station U.S. forces against North Korea? The answers will help indicate how the

[1] National Intelligence Council. "Global Trends 2030: Alternative Worlds." Dec 2012.

dynamics of U.S. – China relations will play out in the Asia-Pacific, a region which overlaps as the new "pivot" of the U.S. and as the backyard of China.

In this paper, I will attempt to answer the following questions. Should the US continue its military alliance with Korea in a post-unification environment? What is the Chinese perspective on the issue? What security arrangement is best for regional stability and for enhancing long-term U.S. - China relations critical for the region and the world?

I will first assess the increasing strategic mistrust in U.S.-China relations in the Asia-Pacific, and evaluate the role of the Korean peninsula as either a crisis point or an opportunity for stability. I will then introduce and evaluate Chinese and Korean debates on the optimal security arrangement of a unified Korean peninsula. Afterwards, I will propose a framework for choosing optimal U.S. policy, evaluate the different policy options, and make a policy proposal. Finally, I will address possible rebuttals and issues for further research.

"Two Speeds"

Deng Xiaoping famously stated that there are "two speeds" in economic development: one for the coast and another for the interior. U.S.-China relations in the Asia-Pacific also seem to have two speeds: one for cooperation and another for competition. In terms of cooperation, it is no overstatement that the bilateral relationship is vastly different from the relationship between the U.S and the Soviet Union during the Cold War. Both Beijing and Washington are linked through common interests such as global economic prosperity and regional stability, institutional engagement such as the Strategic and Economic Dialogue and regular summit meetings, and the vast scale of economic interdependence. As for now, it is in neither country's interest to cripple what many analysts call the most important bilateral relation of today. China expert Kenneth Lieberthal observes that most American policy-makers desire a long-term cooperative relationship between the two major powers, working together in providing public goods such as maritime security and a healthy environment.[2]

---

[2] Lieberthal, Kenneth and Wang Jisi. "Addressing US-China Strategic Distrust". John L. Thornton China Center Monograph Series. 4 (Mar 2012), 20.

Similarly, China's policymakers also understand that the nation's rapid growth and domestic challenges require a non-confrontational relation with the world's main superpower. Premier Wen Jiabao's words that "our common interests far outweigh our differences" is an accurate summary of the current state of Sino-U.S. relations.

The U.S. government's "Pivot to Asia" does not undercut the need for cooperation. Although there are certainly elements that can be perceived as a containment strategy, the core pronouncements associated with the pivot — Secretary Clinton's article America's Pacific Century, the Pentagon's January Defense Strategic Guidelines, and Secretary Panetta's Shangri-La speech — do not undermine the importance of cooperation. Rather, they all acknowledge the need for a cooperative bilateral relation to assure peace and stability in East Asia.

The Chinese response on the official level has also been informal. China's Foreign Ministry and the People's Liberation Army have often responded with the usual rhetorical that they "support the constructive role played by the U.S. in the Asia-Pacific"; and that American joint exercises should be "conducive to the peace and stability of the region"[3] For people who expected an exchange of diplomatic flares, Foreign Minister Yang Jiechi's statement that China is "ready to work with the United States and other countries in this region to develop an Asia-Pacific region that enjoys greater stability and development" was a surprise.[4]

Strategic Mistrust:
Perceptions, Relative Capacities, and Regional Order

However, what they anticipated may be coming. Indeed, the speed of competition may be exceeding the speed of cooperation in the Asia-Pacific. Beneath the web of interactions, an increasing strategic distrust between the two countries has been building up. In what follows, I identify sources of mistrust in perception, relative capability, and regional order. Because both the U.S. and the PRC view the Korean peninsula within the framework of their respective Asia-Pacific strategies, understanding of these elements will be pivotal in resolving the Korea question.

---

[3] Swaine, Michael. "Chinese Leadership and Elite Responses to the U.S. Pacific Pivot." *China Leadership Monitor*. No.38, 9.
[4] Ministry of Foreign Affairs of the People's Republic of China. "Foreign Minister Yang Jiechi Answers Questions from Domestic and Overseas Journalists on China's Foreign Policy and External Relations." (7 Mar 12). Web.

From the American perspective, there is an increasing consensus that China is taking a zero-sum perspective in Sino-U.S. relations. A growing number of Chinese analysts and policymakers express that as China becomes the world's number two, the number one power will counterbalance growing Chinese power. Such thoughts will induce China to counterbalance American influence and eventually overtake the U.S. as the world's supreme power. According to Kenneth Lieberthal, American intelligence communities have gathered information indicating that within internal communications, high-level officials assume a zero-sum attitude in issues related to bilateral relations.[5] Such views are widespread within the Chinese media as well.

Zero-sum perceptions seep into the realm of relative capabilities. Beijing oversees annual double-digit growth in military spending – a massive modernization effort that Washington fears is targeted against American military platforms.[6] The Pentagon's Defense Strategic Guidelines published last January describes China as a "sophisticated adversar[y]" that can use "electronic and cyber warfare, ballistic and cruise missiles, advanced air defenses, mining, and other methods" to deny U.S. forces freedom of access and operation. Beijing has further developed its anti-carrier missile, named the DF-21D, that, in the words of a Pentagon official, can "threaten our primary means of projecting power: our bases, our sea and air assets, and the networks that support them"[7] According to Robert Willard, former commander of the U.S. Pacific Command (PACOM), the challenge to American forces is amplified by the fact that China has an integrated system of ballistic missiles, air-defense systems, and naval systems, including a submarine fleet.[8] Moreover, the buildup raises more suspicion because of the lack of transparency in the interests and goals of the PLA. White Papers published by the People's Liberation Army, for example, do not specify what interests it has in which areas. Strategic trust requires that nations understand each other's long-term goals, and act accordingly and predictably. These elements are noticeably lacking in today's U.S.-China relations.[9] Former PACOM

---

[5] Lieberthal, Kenneth and Wang Jisi. "Addressing US-China Strategic Distrust". John L. Thornton China Center Monograph Series. 4 (Mar 2012), 31.
[6] Ibid, 30
[7] Gertz, Bill. "China has carrier-killer missile, U.S. admiral says." The Washington Times. December 27, 2010. Web.
[8] Ibid.,
[9] Lieberthal, Kenneth and Wang Jisi. "Addressing US-China Strategic Distrust". John L. Thornton China Center Monograph Series. 4 (Mar 2012), 30.

Commander Robert Willard's testimony at Congress that China's military modernization is not harmonious with the Chinese policy of the "harmonious world" can be understood in this context.[10]

Finally, in terms of regional order, the U.S. has seen an increasingly heavyweight China possibly pushing back against the established order in the Asia-Pacific. One phenomenon is Chinese assertiveness against American-led alliance systems.[11] In 2010, for example, Beijing vociferously opposed the U.S.-South Korea naval exercise in the Yellow Sea after North Korea torpedoed a South Korean warship. The same year, Foreign Minister Yang Jiechi warned Washington not to intervene in the South China Sea dispute, making the infamous statement that "China is a big country and other countries are small countries, and that's just a fact."[12] After the ASEAN conference this September, the Chinese Foreign Ministry criticized the U.S. for taking sides in the South China Sea despite claims of neutrality, while the state-run Xinhua newspaper proclaimed less diplomatically that "[t]he United States should stop its role as a sneaky trouble maker sitting behind some nations in the region and pulling strings."[13] Last December, after the U.S. Senate passed an amendment acknowledging Japan's administration of the disputed Senkaku/Diaoyu islands, Foreign Ministry Spokesperson Hong Lei criticized the U.S.-Japan security treaty as "a product of the Cold War."[14]

the Chinese Perspective

Then would do the Chinese think? In terms of perception, just as many Americans see a zero-sum attitude in the Chinese, the Chinese see a zero-sum attitude in the Americans. An increasing number of Chinese analysts believe that the U.S. aim is to maintain its supremacy. And China — a large, rising nation with very different politics, values, and culture — would be the main challenge. In a recent Foreign Affairs Article, Nathan and Scobell argue that there is a rising consensus within different groups of Chinese thinkers – traditional Marxists who see the U.S. as an imperial power, young realist scholars who follow the power transition theory, and cultural royalists who emphasize the primacy of Chinese culture –

[10] Santis, Hughe De. "The China Threat and the "Pivot" to Asia." Current History. (September 2012), 212.
[11] Ibid., 27
[12] Pomfret, John. "U.S. takes a tougher tone with China". The Washington Post. 30 Jul 12. Web.
[13] Chang, Liu. "Washington needs to take concrete steps to promote China-U.S. ties." China Daily. 4 Sep 12. Web.
[14] "China condemns Senkaku amendment to U.S.-Japan security treaty." The Japan Times. 4 Dec 12.

that America is maintaining its power at the cost of China.[15] David Shambaugh, after identifying schools of thinking in Chinese foreign policy, points out that the center of gravity for Chinese foreign policy strategists is increasingly tilting toward Marxist and realist thinking, both of which warn against possible U.S. exploitation and aggression.[16]

Recently, Chinese strategists have perceived disturbing American pressure both within and outside of the PRC. In the domestic realm, American support for civil societies and political liberalization, criticisms against human rights, and presidential meetings with the Dalai Lama are often seen as attacks on the iron grip of the Chinese Communist Party. In terms of foreign policy, the U.S. is enacting what one analysts calls a "strategic ring of encirclement", enhancing military cooperation with China's neighbors: west from Kyrgyzstan to India, south from Burma to Australia (and of course Taiwan), and East to South Korea and Japan. Fueling the tension is the close-in surveillance activities of American spyplanes and ships, which sometimes venture so close to the Chinese coastline that they alarm the PLA.[17] As Chinese strategist Wang Jisi points out, no other country in the world, even Russia, is the target of such "daily American military pressure."[18]

The recent pivot to Asia has largely exacerbated such anxieties. Not only will the U.S. strengthen its alliances with current allies in the region – Japan, South Korea, Indonesia, Phillipines, and Thailand – it will bolster partnerships with key nations – India, Singapore, Indonesia – and focus sixty percent of its navy in the Asia-Pacific by 2020 – including six aircraft carriers and a majority of cruisers, destroyers, and submarines. The majority of Chinese analysts perceive that China is the target, and criticize that in an economically dynamic region, the U.S. is trying to reap economic benefits while politically containing China's growing power.[19] For example, in response to the U.S. Defense Strategic Guidance this January, Major General Luo Yan wrote in the Liberation Army Daily that "[c]asting our eyes around we can see that the United States has been bolstering its five major military alliances in the Asia-Pacific

[15] Nathan, Andrew and Andrew Scobell. "How China Sees America." 91. (Sep/Oct 2012): 97-104. Web.
[16] Shambaugh, David. "Coping with a Conflicted China." Washington Quarterly. 34.1 (Winter2010/2011), 25.
[17] Lieberthal, Kenneth and Wang Jisi. "Addressing US-China Strategic Distrust". John L. Thornton China Center Monograph Series. 4 (Mar 2012), 28
[18] Ibid.
[19] Swaine, Michael. "Chinese Leadership and Elite Responses to the U.S. Pacific Pivot." China Leadership Monitor. No.38., 6.

region, and is adjusting the positioning of its five major military base clusters, while also seeking more entry rights for military bases around China. Who can believe that you are not directing this at China"?[20]

Next, in terms of capability, many Chinese believe that the U.S. is a declining power.[21] In economics, for example, the 2008 Financial Crisis that originated in Wall Street was an indication that the U.S.-led international financial architecture contains serious flaws. In politics, the Chinese leadership is observing an increasingly partisan culture incapable to deal with pressing issues such as rising debt, economic recovery, welfare, and infrastructure. During beginning of the Iraq War, the U.S. GDP was eight times larger than China; now it is less than 3 times as large.[22] Meanwhile, the financial crisis and the prolonged wars in Iraq and Afghanistan coincided with growing Chinese power. In 2007, China surpassed Germany as the world's third largest economy, Japan in 2010 as the second largest, and will probably surpass the United States in 2016.[23] In 2008, when the U.S. and Europe were in dismay after the 2008 Economic Crisis, China became the first country to recover and boosted global demand. The same year, Beijing celebrated the most lavish Olympics ever.

With growing capabilities, Beijing is growing wary of the status-quo regional order. To better understand Chinese view of geopolitics, we can pretend to take Xi Jingping's seat at the CCP Standing Committee conference room and take out a map. From the west to the southwest is positioned the U.S. Central Command, which still maintains some troops in Afghanistan and has access to an airbase in Kyrgyzstan.[24] To the south, India, which is closely aligning with Washington as part of the pivot, has recently announced that it could dispatch its navy to the South China Sea.[25] To the South and Southeast, Myanmar, Vietnam, Singapore, and Australia have aligned closer with the United States, while the latter three will enhance military cooperation through joint exercises, arms purchases, and increased U.S. force deployment. The geostrategic southeast sea-lane is also blocked by Taiwan, which

---

[20] Buckley, Chris. "China top military paper warns U.S. aims to contain rise." *Reuters*. 10 Jan 12.

[21] Lieberthal, Kenneth and Wang Jisi. "Addressing US-China Strategic Distrust". John L. Thornton China Center Monograph Series. 4 (Mar 2012), 9.

[22] Ibid.

[23] "China's Economy picking up steam." China Daily. 26 Nov 2012. Web.

[24] Nathan, Andrew and Andrew Scobell. "How China Sees America." 91. (Sep/Oct 2012): 97-104. Web.

[25] Jaishankar, Dhruva. "India's Ocean: Could New Delhi's growing naval force change the balance of power in the Pacific?" Foreign Policy. 6 Dec 12. Web.

Robert Kaplan calls "the Great Wall in reverse", preventing China from expanding beyond the Taiwan Strait.[26] Further east are the approximately 75,000 troops stationed in South Korea and Japan. In the background is the U.S. Pacific Command, which wields the largest manpower and widest operation range among America's six regional commands.[27]

Of course, Washington has asserted that it will protect the global commons, support an open Asia-Pacific for the development for all, and has never attacked Chinese mainland. Nevertheless, switching shoes, if Mexico, a Chinese military ally, has PLA troops stationed south of California; if Puerto Rico, another military ally, receives advanced Chinese arms despite the "One America Policy", and if the PLA, freely projecting force in the Atlantic and Pacific, maneuvers advanced carrier fleets near America's east and west coasts, would not Washington want to push back if it had the power?

Disentangling the Gordian Knot

In sum, the U.S., for its part, does not necessarily consider China as an enemy, unless one wants to start another conflict in Asia. Nevertheless, because Washington is unsure of Beijing's ultimate intentions, any assertion of interest by Beijing is bound to be received as assertiveness. Combined with a closing gap in relative capabilities and occasional cries of agony against U.S. led bilateral alliances, China can be seen as a revisionist power that will not play by our rules. In contrast, for Beijing, the U.S.-led order in the Asia-Pacific itself contributes to their zero-sum thinking that they are encircled by America and its allies. Now that China is growing stronger, it is using its abilities to slowly assert its interest and push back against what they see as a Cold-War style bilateral alliance system. Thus, although both recognize, very strongly, the need for establishing a working relationship between the world's two strongest countries, each perceives the other as provocative.[28] Therefore solving this Gordian knot requires the U.S. to explain that its alliance systems (and recent partnerships) in the region are not a threat to China while China should explain its long-term goals and interests.

[26] Kaplan, Robert D. "The Geography of Chinese Power: How Far Can Beijing Reach on Land and at Sea?" Foreign Affairs. May/Jun 2010. Web.

[27] Nathan, Andrew and Andrew Scobell. "How China Sees America." 91. (Sep/Oct 2012): 97-104. Web.

[28] Swaine, Michael. "Perceptions of an Assertive China." *China Leadership Monitor*. No.32., 9.

This is where the Korean peninsula comes in. Whether to assuage the growing number of pundits who predict zero-sum competition, or to help solve the sources of mistrust stated above, the Korean peninsula can be an opportunity for U.S.-China relations.

The Korean Peninsula

The Korean peninsula is unique region in that American and Chinese interests clash head-on along the 38th parallel. Washington and China both have core interests in the peninsula. The PRC sacrificed hundreds of thousands of soldiers during the Korean War, and continues to support the Pyongyang regime even at the cost of international pressure and stigma. The U.S. has also lost tens of thousands of soldiers during the war, and still deploys about 30,000 troops in South Korea. The separation of the Korean peninsula into the North and South, supported by two rival powers, is a symbol that neither Washington nor Beijing is willing to handover influence over the entire peninsula to its rival.

A consequence is that the Korean peninsula will be a key region in gauging the prospects of future U.S.-China relations. When the two Koreas eventually reunite, the status-quo that has allowed both nations to have their spheres of influence in the peninsula will fall. China will inevitably lose its own buffer zone above the 38th parallel, while the U.S. will lose legitimacy in stationing tens of thousands of troops in the peninsula. China's fears of a strategic encirclement will ignite if the U.S. continues a bilateral military alliance with a unified Korea. Meanwhile, the Koreans for their part will have to make a choice on whether to continue the alliance or not, and under what conditions. Indeed, how these nations handle the issue of post-unification security regime will be an important part of how the U.S. and China manage changing power dynamics in the world's most economically vibrant yet politically tense region. How far will Beijing push for increased influence, and how will Washington adjust the established order to fit a stronger China? Will Washington and Beijing play a scramble for allies?

Chinese Consensus: Not in My Backyard

The majority view among Chinese strategists is that once the Koreas are reunified, the U.S. must leave as well. Any extension of the U.S.-ROK security treaty to the entire peninsula is viewed an obvious American attempt to contain China. Although Chinese opinion on foreign policy is generally divided among different

schools of thought, they seem to reach consensus on this point. Realists such as Yan Xuetong oppose American presence across the Yalu river border, and even call for China to extend its influence on the peninsula to counter-balance U.S. presence (Yan).[29] Wang Jisi from the great powers school also argues that in the short-term, the US alliance is acceptable; in the long-term, it must be replaced by a regional security regime.[30] Zheng Bijian, the formulator of the official peaceful rise policy, argues that in a post-Cold War world, China and the U.S. should establish a collective security regime to foster cooperation, rather than continue Cold War style, competitive bilateral alliances.[31] Others such as Jia Qingquo argue that if Sino-US relations deteriorate, the Chinese will hope that a unified Korea will be on Beijing's side.[32] The consensus among most Chinese analysts is a neutralized Korea with a pact among neighboring powers to respect its neutrality.[33] Beijing's key objective on the peninsula is to secure a strategic buffer, and neutralization is the Beijing-style of "a political reconfiguration of the region that is poised to reduce, if not exclude, the U.S. presence."[34]

The Chinese are well-versed in the geopolitics between Beijing, Northeast China, and the Korean peninsula. A long-held geostrategic perception is that, as an ancient metaphor from Tang China states, the Korean peninsula is like "a hammer poised to strike China's head". Korea, either when occupied by a regime hostile to China, or when under the influence of a regional hegemon, is an important geostrategic foothold to threaten or strike Manchuria. If Manchuria is taken, Beijing is within easy distance of a hostile power.

East Asian history provides numerous examples stretching back centuries. In the 13th century, before the Mongols conquered

[29] Yan, Xuetong. "How China Can Defeat America" The New York Times
[30] Wang, Jisi. "Chungguk ŭi daemi chŏngch'aek – hyŏmnyŏk vs. taehang (Chinese Policy toward the US – Cooperation v. Conflict)." Chungguk ŭi naeilŭl mutda (Question the Future of China). Ed. Moon, Jung In. (Seoul: Samsung Economic Research Institute, 2010) 123.
[31] Zheng, Bijian. "Hwap'yŏnggulgi – Chungguk wihyŏbrongwa punggoeronŭl nŏmŏsŏ (Peaceful Rise – Beyond Theories of the Chinese Threat and the Chinese Collapse)." Chungguk ŭi naeilŭl mutda (Question the Future of China). Ed. Moon, Jung In. (Seoul: Samsung Economic Research Institute, 2010) 31.
[32] Jia, Qinguo. "21-segiŭi chunggukgwa han'guk (China and Korea in the 21st Century)." Chungguk ŭi naeilŭl mutda (Question the Future of China). Ed. Moon, Jung In. (Seoul: Samsung Economic Research Institute, 2010) 213.
[33] Snyder, Scott. "Value and Significance of Korean Reunification within the Dynamics of Northeast Asia." SERI Quarterly 4.1 (2011), 69.
[34] Wang, Jisi. "Chungguk ŭi daemi chŏngch'aek – hyŏmnyŏk vs. taehang (Chinese Policy toward the US – Cooperation v. Conflict)." Chungguk ŭi naeilŭl mutda (Question the Future of China). Ed. Moon, Jung In. (Seoul: Samsung Economic Research Institute, 2010), 135.

China's Song Dynasty, they first subdued Korea's Koryo Dynasty out of fear that a Korea loyal to China could strike Manchuria from behind. The same patter occurred several centuries later when the Manchus – who established the Qing Dynasty – similarly subdued Korea's Chosun Dynasty before conquering Chinese mainland, and forced Korea to sever its ties to China. In 1592, when Japanese troops marched toward the Yalu river upon invading Korea, China's Ming Dynasty dispatched tens of thousands of soldiers to Korea's aid. The economic woes of the Ming at the time did not prevent them from mass military deployment, because they feared that a hostile Japan can overtake Manchuria, and attempt conquest of China.

Their nightmare scenario came true in the early to mid-20th century. Imperial Japan took over Manchuria en-route Korea and launched an invasion into China, starting the second Sino-Japanese War. The war, which witnessed atrocities such as the Nanjing Massacre, would end only with the surrender of Japan after the nuclear bombing of Hiroshima and Nagasaki.

Five years later, it was China that would use the peninsula to protect its interests. Several months into the Korea War, as Douglas McArthur's troops marched victoriously toward the Yalu River border, Mao dispatched his 1-million strong army to defend North Korea from destruction. Although there is ongoing debate on the calculus of major actors such as Mao Zedong, Douglas McArthur, and Harry Truman, mainstream theory suggests that the overwhelming impulse of China was to protect their strategic buffer, and prevent the war from expanding into the Manchuria theater.

If Xi Jinping or any of his successive leaders asks the Korea expert about the geopolitics of the peninsula, the adviser will likely remember these among innumerable instances in which China lost hundreds of thousands of lives to prevent the peninsula from falling into the hands of a rival power. Of course, the U.S. troops stationed in the peninsula will not likely engage in another war in the Asian mainland. Nevertheless, with such history and geopolitics, the presence of foreign troops itself can be a source of threat in the hearts of the Beijing leadership. Perception ultimately rests upon Beijing – if Chinese strategists stare deep into the peninsula, they will see American strategists staring back into them.

Fueling the geopolitical concern are Chinese perceptions of an American "strategic ring of encirclement." As mentioned earlier, from China's west to south to east, except its nothern

border with Russia and northeastern border with North Korea, Beijing is enveloped by American allies, partners, or military bases. From the Chinese perspective, it is only natural that they would preserve whatever buffer zone they already have. Wang Fei Ling, for example, states that this is why Chinese analysts have recently "started to semi-openly talk about the rising strategic value of North Korea as seemingly the only way to prevent an otherwise inevitable and fatal full-moon encirclement of China by the United States."[35]

China's Strategic Minorities: I'm Not Afraid of Foggy Bottom

However, there are dissenting Chinese views as well, although most scholars in China, Korea, and the US suggest that they are a minority. Wang Feiling argues that since the 1990s, Beijing no longer believes that a U.S. presence is aimed at China. American troops are "not a threatening force, but it's still a bargaining chip" for China.[36] On the contrary, some Chinese officials support continued U.S. influence to "at least keep the Koreans under control."[37] Such thinking may reflect that China has shifted from playing a zero-sum scramble for allies to directly managing regional affairs upon a partnership with the U.S. Perhaps what worries Beijing is not that the U.S. would recklessly seek a conflict with the second world power, but rather that a possible surge of nationalism within a unified Korea will ignite territorial conflicts or nationalist clashes. Chinese scholar Zhang Yunling also mentions that China is confident in Sino-US relations and no longer needs a buffer zone in the peninsula.[38]

However, Korean analysts rebut that the current South Korean administration has always been engaged in wishful thinking in regards to North Korea and China. Despite several dissenting views, the majority argument among Chinese officials and analysts is that the alliance must end upon reunification. Moreover, recent Chinese support of North Korea such as a swift embrace of the hereditary succession, protection from international sanctions after

[35] Wang, Fei-Ling. "Status Quo Reassessed: China's Shifting Views on Korean Unification". US-China Relations and Korean Unification. Ed. Choi, Jinwook. (Seoul: Korean Institute of Nation al Unification, 2012.), 156.

[36] Ibid., 172.

[37] Ibid., 171.

[38] Zhang, Yunling. "Chunggukui daechollyakgwa asia chiyokjuui (Chinese Grand Strategy and Regionalism in Asia)." Chunggukui naeilul mutda (Question the Future of China). Ed. Moon, Jung In. (Seoul: Samsung Economic Research Institute, 2010.), 176.

provocations in 2010, and continuing aid suggest otherwise. In combination with recent Chinese assertiveness in the Asia-Pacific, the PRC's continuous embrace of North Korea appears to confirm that the Beijing leadership has shifted to a strategy of maintaining Chinese influence, or at least decreasing American influence, on the peninsula.

The Buck Stops at Seoul: For the Alliance

To be sure, the security arrangement on a united Korea will be decided through consultations, negotiations, and mutual accommodation among Washington, Seoul, and Beijing. Nevertheless, the decision of a country whether to continue an alliance or not will depend much on the will of the country's public and leadership. In this section, I will examine the currents debates in Seoul, evaluate the different arguments, and identify variables that will affect Korean decisions.

The current mainstream view is to continue the alliance. According to this argument, the optimal choice for a unified Korea is to ally with an offshore balancer – the United States – that can balance the power of Korea against the stronger China, Japan, and Russia. Proponents argue that Koreans cannot yet trust China as a reliable neighboring partner. The idea of a Chinese threat is present in Korea, where many people remember that throughout history, whenever China became stronger, it threatened or invaded Korea. With the rise of China, many Koreans are wary of what they perceive as Beijing's increasing assertiveness, especially in 2010 with Chinese claims to the South China Sea and its maritime dispute over a fishing boat caught in Japanese waters. Especially in the latter, the pressure that China exerted on Japan, including the export ban on rare-earth materials and suspension of tourism, received high media coverage in South Korea as a symbol of rising Chinese assertiveness.

Direct conflicts and nationalistic emotions also limit the relationship between Korea and China. A well-publicized conflict was China's historical claims over the history of the Kokuryu and Balhae Kingdoms in Manchuria, which Koreans claim as their own. The claim led to fierce nationalistic sentiments on both publics and ignited fears in South Korea that China is either setting the stage to absorb North Korea or to prevent a future unified Korea from making territorial claims on its ancient land. A more recent source of alarm was China's perceived backing of North Korea after the sinking of the Cheonan warship and the shelling of Yeonpyeong island. China was portrayed as a selfish and irresponsible partner,

and Koreans lowered the hope they had for a responsible Chinese partner. Proponents of alliance would thus point out that Korea's relation with China is replete with conflict including territorial disputes, rivalry, and historical mistrust, none of which are present with Seoul's relation with Washington. As long as they persist, an alliance with the U.S. is the best bet.

In contrast, Washington is a much more reliable ally. To many Korean analysts, the United States is the perceived as the only power with interests in the peninsula that does not have territorial ambitions. This is not to say that China or Japan has plans for an attack, but Koreans are nonetheless wary of the innumerable invasions from China and Japan throughout their history. For a mid-power country surrounded by even stronger nations, a superpower that can act an offshore balancer is the optimal choice.

Another aspect is values. Especially among South Korean conservatives, the idea that the shared values of democracy, human rights, market economy should guide alliance policy is gaining track. The Chinese Communist Party does not share these values, which add a layer of doubt in Seoul. The recent outreach efforts by Seoul such as hosting the G20 and the Nuclear Summit are also signs that Korea shares liberal values with the US, and that the alliance will help Korea to pursue a global role that it desires.

An important assumption underlying the argument for a continued US alliance is that Korea-US relations and Korea-China relations are not zero-sum but rather policies that can be pursued in parallel.[39] Many strategists agree that upon a Korea-US alliance, Seoul can and should promote better relations with neighboring countries without leaving out either Washington or Beijing.

Proponents of a US alliance also point out problems with neutralizing the peninsula. The crux of their argument is that neutralization is not a reliable method for security, for it relies upon a pact with the stronger neighbors which Korea cannot trust.[40] Without an ally, if neutralization collapses for whatever reason, Korea will be left at the mercy of its powerful neighbor. To be fair, a unified Korea will not be a weak military power, but it will be weaker than the US, China, Japan, and Russia. Meanwhile, the public will be doubtful of relying on a pact with these four powers for security.

[39] Yoon, Young Kuan. "Hanbandoui Miraerrul Malhada (The Future of the Korean Peninsula)." Sinnyonkihoek t'ukchip Daet'oron (New Year's Special Grand Discussion). KBS. 15 Jan.2011. Television. Discussion.
[40] Kang, Kwang Suk. *Joongriphwa wua hanabando t'ongil* (Neutralization and Korean Unification), 12. (Seoul: Baeksan. 2010), 9.

Neutralization also relies on the motivations of the regional powers – it can be a thinly disguised veil for a state to temporarily move out of the contested region only to return later when it is stronger.[41] For example, China may agree to neutralize the peninsula only because it is weaker than the United States, but destroy the agreement and impose its influence once it perceives that it can match the power of Washington. The fears of neutralization are also worsened by the fact that there has been no precedence of neutralization in East Asian history.[42] Worries that neutralization cannot guarantee security are pronounced especially because Korea has seen many of its Kingdoms collapse from foreign invasions.

Challenging Opinion: Support for Neutralization

Meanwhile, proponents of neutralization argue with powerful logic as well. The idea starts with a strategic assessment of Korean geopolitics. The peninsula is located in an important crossroad linking the Pacific Ocean with the Eurasian landmass, the faultline between major land-based powers such as China and Russia, and major sea-based powers such as Japan and the US.[43] As a result, Korea has always been the stage for competing societies. In the pre-modern era, semi-nomadic societies such as the Mongols and the Manchus invaded Korea before conquering China. In more recent history, the peninsula has been the theater of war between naval power Japan and land power China in the 1st Sino-Japanese War, between naval power Japan and land power Russia in the Russo-Japanese War, and between naval power U.S. and land power PRC in the Korean War. For any state wanting to either expand into or protect the pacific or Eurasia, the Korean peninsula was a key pathway.

The logic that Korean analysts draw from this experience is that all surrounding countries must secure or at least prevent the peninsula from falling into another's sphere of influence. They often cite the above metaphor that the Korean peninsula is a hammer that strikes the head of China, and the Japanese metaphor that it is a dagger pointing at the heart of Japan. The historical theme can be seen ever more clearly in today's separated Korea. This time, two great powers have ostensibly divided the peninsula into their own strategic buffers and spheres of influence. Thus, Korea has often been the victim of great power politics; naturally, the solution is to insulate it from the foreign competitions that have bedeviled its history.

[41] Ibid, 12.

[42] Ibid., 51.

[43] Bae, Ki Chan. K'oria, Tasi Saengjonui Kiroe Soda (Korea, Again on the Crossroads of Survival). (Seoul: Wisdom House, 2005), 52.

It is upon this understanding insight of Korea's relation to the world that some strategists argue for neutralization. They assert that neutralization is best suitable for states "in which two or more external actors have substantial and competitive interests" or "that by reason of strategic or symbolic political value, become the focal of contests for control or dominant influence between principal regional or global rivals."[44] Neutralization is also suitable for countries that are divided or can serve as a bridge between more powerful states.[45] Korea is a suitable match.

Finally, proponents for neutralization argue that it is beneficial to all parties involved. Neutrality is often used to respond to a change in the status quo, avoid conflict, and conclude international disputes. Amidst the uncertainty of Korean reunification, neutrality can bring results that can satisfy everybody. For Washington, it can prevent a unified Korea from falling into a growing China's sphere of influence, a long-term possibility which American strategists such as Brzezinski have worried about. For China, it can expand its buffer zone against the Unite States to the entire peninsula. For Korea, it can gain the legitimacy to act as an independent mediator in the region, a role that Switzerland and Austria enjoys. A unified Korea can position itself as a mediator between China and Japan, a role which the Chinese would welcome. Furthermore, Korea may continue to take on a more global role in fields such as finance, environment, democracy, poverty reduction, and conflict mediation after its security is guaranteed against surrounding superpowers. Some Koreans envision that because they will have experienced and overcome colonialism, war, ideology, industrialization, democratization, and eventually denuclearization and national division, they will take on an active role to support countries that suffer from those problems. Such a role would be desirable for the Koreans, Americans, and Chinese alike.

The argument for a neutralized Korea is supported among liberals, students, the younger generation, and supporters of the sunshine policy. There are also think-tanks and organizations committed to neutralized reunification. The young generation may be especially supportive in the future, for they have no memory of the Korean War or the anti-communist military dictatorships. They may also be sensitive to the perceived lack of sovereignty that the alliance brings; for example, troops to Iraq, sanctions against Iran, and huge US army bases in downtown Seoul.

[44] Koh, B. C. "[Untitled]." The American Political Science Review 75.3 (1981): pp. 832-833. Web.
[45] Kang, Jong Il. "A Study on Korean Peninsula Reunification Via Permanent Neutrality." The Korean Journal of International Relations 41.1 (2001), 35.

Washington's Optimal Policy

Then what should be the optimal policy for Washington? To be sure, Korea's security regime will be decided among a close consultation between Washington, Beijing, and Seoul. All have the legitimacy to have their voice heard. China has supported North Korea since the Cold War, and has legitimate concerns about security in its backyard. Korea is the party that has been the victim of the separation regime since the Cold War and must make a sovereign decision on its future. The U.S. has supported South Korea since the Cold War, and is currently the prominent power in the Asia-Pacific. All are parties that have created the separation regime; they must work together to create a new order upon unification.

Thus, Washington has a significant stake to formulate its own position. A key concern for the United States is the establishment of a stable regional order in the context of a rising China; how far it is willing to accommodate China's rise and adjust the Asia-Pacific order. In the context of rising strategic mistrust, unification will pose a challenge, or become an opportunity for, the U.S. and China to find a joint interest that can satisfy both parties. To do so, the security regime on the peninsula must address the gap in mutual mistrust between the U.S. and China. I will evaluate each of the options in respect to perception, relative capabilities, and regional order.

In terms of perception, continuing the military reliance is likely to fuel the existing security dilemma between the two nations. As discussed above, the majority of Chinese analysts oppose U.S. influence on its borders, for understandable geopolitical concerns. The Chinese perception is that without the North Korean threat, the only possible purpose of U.S. troops is to contain China's growing influence — any other rationale such as regional stability is a poison apple.[46] Some Chinese analysts have even gone further to declare that a continued alliance is unacceptable "unless these links were part of an anti-Japanese alignment with Seoul and Beijing", a demand (or a satire) that the U.S. would not agree to.[47]

If the U.S. continues the alliance, not only would Beijing perceive a threat, it would also firmly confirm its zero-sum perception against the U.S. Unless the Korean peninsula allies with both China and the U.S., a bilateral military alliance with one party will likely exclude the other from political and military influence. Should the Chinese perceive that the U.S. is pivoting its foot in a unified Korea

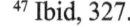

[46] Harrison, Selig S. Korean Endgame : A Strategy for Reunification and U.S. Disengagement. Princeton, N.J.: Princeton University Press, 2002, 326.
[47] Ibid, 327.

to counterbalance China, zero-sum thinking will pervade in Chinese foreign policy circles, dampening the prospects of future U.S.-China cooperation. As Joseph Nye warns, "If we treated China as an enemy, we were guaranteeing an enemy in the future. If we treated China as a friend, we could not guarantee friendship, but we could at least keep open the possibility of more benign outcomes."[48]

Then what will happen with neutralization? Neutralizing the peninsula will result in both parties renouncing its political-military influence in the region. Thus, it will not incur a security dilemma, and will satisfy Beijing's hopes to continue a strategic buffer and also Washington's hopes to prevent Korea from falling into China's sphere of influence. Washington and Beijing will eliminate a source of competition, while cooperation will likely be strengthened as the parties collaborate in neutralizing the peninsula.

As for capabilities, although Washington may want to counterbalance the decreasing power gap through a renewed alliance with Korea, it is doubtful whether it can succeed. There is an inherent contradiction at work: because of growing Chinese power the U.S. hopes to shore up alliances in the region, but in the long-run, bilateral alliances may not be sustainable for the same reason. One reason is that China has more at stake. Situated on China's border, the Korean peninsula has been a geostrategic foothold throughout history. Preventing a rival power from accessing the peninsula is directly related to China's security, but not for the U.S. The peninsula is several thousand miles apart from American mainland, and despite its geopolitical value, it is not immediately related to America's territorial security. Thus, it is only natural for China to oppose the alliance, even more so as it decreases the power gap vis-a-vis the United States.

Another worry is that should a new U.S.-unified Korea alliance system be set up, China will lash back through provocations. Chinese strategist Zhu Feng argues that a continuation of the Washington-Tokyo-Seoul link will be "detrimental to maintaining peace in Northeast Asia" and only induce "troubling behavior from Beijing."[49] For example, he warns that in case of a Sino-U.S. conflict, American troops stationed near the Yalu border will be decimated. In addition, Korea will be considered as an anti-China foothold, and a China-Korea conflict will only add more tensions to a region already replete with rivalry and competition.[50]

[48] Nye, Joseph. "Should China be Contained?" CNN. 4 Jul 11. Web.
[49] Zhu, Feng. "Unification of Two Koreas: On View of China." Twenty Years after German Unification and Preparing for Korean Unification. Korean Institute for National Unification. Lotte Hotel, Seoul. 5 Oct. 2010. Presentation II.
[50] Dujarric, R. "Korea After Unification: An Opportunity to Strengthen the Korean-

Meanwhile, a neutral Korean peninsula also begs several questions as well. If successful, neutralization will prevent the long-term strategic possibility that the peninsula will fall into the Chinese sphere of influence. However, there are also legitimate concerns of a power vacuum should the U.S. troops leave. Without American presence, the Korean peninsula will be open to Chinese assertiveness, either through territorial disputes or through Beijing's pressure to force Korea to succumb to its interests in the region.[51] In such a scenario, Washington will also take the blame for leaving the peninsula, and its commitment to allies will be questioned.

However, the possibility of a power vacuum will be complicated by a firm Korean resistance against Chinese assertiveness. Many Koreans harbor a perception of the Chinese and are aware of the territorial disputes, historical issues, and nationalism between the countries. Furthermore, Beijing would likely calculate that as long as Korea does not fall into the U.S. sphere of influence, the optimal strategy is to maintain good relations. Should it attempt to break a neutrality pact and intervene in Korea, not only will it incur the hostility of the world's top ten economic and military power, it will also provide the U.S. will the legitimacy to step in to Korea's aid. Once in motion, Beijing will face a hostile unified Korea aligned with the U.S. in addition to the myriad of problems such as Taiwan and Japan – certainly not what the leadership needs. China's leading strategist Zheng Bijian confirms that "Beijing understands that improving relations with a unified Korea is more beneficial than taking the unbearable risk of uncertainty through intervention."[52]

Finally, in terms of the regional order, a renewed U.S.-unified Korea alliance will tighten what Beijing perceives as a strategic ring of encirclement. China's Yalu river border with North Korea is the only border, except the border with Russia, that currently does not have a U.S. presence. The Chinese, as they have already done so recently, will publicly question the purpose of the alliance, criticize it as representing a Cold-War mentality, and display provocative behavior such as assertive territorial

American Partnership." Korean Journal of Defense Analysis 12.1 (2000), 45.
[51] Walt, Stephen. "Explaining Obama' s Asia Policy." A realist in an ideological age. Foreign Policy. Web. 4/5/2012.
[52] Zheng, Bijian. "Hwap'yonggulgi – Chungguk wihyobrongwa punggoeronul nomoso (Peaceful Rise – Beyond Theories of the Chinese Threat and the Chinese Collapse)." Chungguk ui naeilul mutda (Question the Future of China). Ed. Moon, Jung In. (Seoul: Samsung Economic Research Institute, 2010), 39.

claims, dispatching of ships and planes near disputed waters, or harassment of U.S.-Korea joint troops during military exercise. In turn, such actions will induce analysts in Washington to perceive that Beijing in attempting to overturn the established order, and fuel further mistrust.

Neutrality, however, will aim to purposely isolate the peninsula from political influence by either China or the U.S. China will be satisfied once the peninsula is excluded from the U.S.-led bilateral alliance system, for it already has enough problems on its borders. For the U.S., it can maintain regional stability by preventing China from raising tensions against Korea as well as in the case of continued alliance. At a time when tension is escalating over the South China Sea, the disputed waters over the Diaoyu/Senakaku islands, and even with territorial disputes with India, at least one focal point for peace and cooperation will help maintain regional stability in areas where possible.

The issue begs the larger question of the kind of regional order suitable for the Asia-Pacific. Walter Russell Mead argues that we must aim for "a liberal Asian security and economic order that promotes the peaceful development of all the countries in the region."[53] Zbigniew Brzezinski claims that geopolitical equilibrium in 21st century Asia cannot be continuously sustained through power projection by a non-Asian power and external military alliances.[54] David Lampton asserts that we must search for "a security structure such that we all are dedicated to maintaining stability in the region."[55] One of the aims of the Asia pivot as well is a prosperous Asia-Pacific with a free-flow of people, goods, and interaction.

A continuance of bilateral military alliance is unlikely to achieve the above purposes. On the contrary, it will likely induce political tensions, military buildup, and zero-sum thinking in the Asia-Pacific. At least in terms of U.S.-China relations, with emphasis on perception, capability, and regional order, a renewed U.S.-Korea alliance will do more harm than good.

[53] Mead, Walter Russell. "Game of Thrones: US Pushes Naval Buildup In Asia". Via Media. The American Interest. Web. 2 Jun 2012.
[54] Brzezinski, Zbignew. "Balancing the East, Upgrading the West: U.S. Grand Strategy in an Age of Upheaval." Foreign Affairs 91. 1 (Jan/Feb 2012): 97-104. Web.
[55] Lampton, David M. "Beijing, Washington, and the Korean Peninsula". US-China Relations and Korean Unification. Ed. Choi, Jinwook. (Seoul: Korean Institute of Nation al Unification, 2012), 257.

Opposition

This is not to say that neutralization will be a panacea for the Korea problem. Rather, there are legitimate concerns that I will address in this section.

One is that Beijing may use neutralization as cover to maintain a low profile and hide its capacities until it is sure that it can exert its own sphere of influence in the peninsula. Will China continue to respect the neutrality of the peninsula if they can someday match the power of the United States? Although I argued that such attempt by Beijing will elicit a Korean and American response that will further align Asian nations against a rising China, as aptly questioned by David Lampton, "[h]ow dependent do you want to be on Chinese benevolence"?[56]

However, it is also a valid assumption that the Chinese are rational actors acting on nation interest and cost-benefit analysis. The larger goal is not to subdue Korea under its influence in itself, but to become a great, returning power that the Chinese have historically prided on. If China breaks a neutrality pact and attempts to subdue Korea under its influence, the U.S., Japan, ASEAN, India, and possibly even Russia will be alarmed at the aggressiveness, and likely seek a coalition to contain such hostility. In such a scenario, even if China is stronger than most its neighbors one-by-one – also a questionable assumption – it will face a tightening of the strategic ring of encirclement led by the U.S. and joined by Japan, India, Russia, and ASEAN. As for now, even as China's economy is expected to surpass the U.S. in overall GDP terms within a decade, it still lags far behind in overall national power including hard military power, economic power (GDP size is not everything), and soft power. Even in the long-term future, China face challenges such as extreme inequality, a rapidly aging population, provision of welfare for 1.3 billion people, and environmental degradation. Even if it does overcome those problems, it seems unlikely that it will either have the power or the resolve to withstand being isolated by its neighbors. The Chinese are known to be rational and patient calculators; they are unlikely to make a self-defeating move of such magnitude.

Another rests on my assumption that China adamantly opposes a continued alliance. In contrast, some analysts argue that having

[56] Lampton, David M. "Beijing, Washington, and the Korean Peninsula". US-China Relations and Korean Unification. Ed. Choi, Jinwook. (Seoul: Korean Institute of Nation al Unification, 2012), 257.

an alliance per se should not necessarily incur a security dilemma. As John Ikenberry states, "[i]t's important that there be no security dilemma implied in simply having alliances", the issue is with management.[57] The same view is held by Korea specialists, such as Scott Snyder and Victor Cha, who emphasize the need for a strategic dialogue between Washington, Beijing, and Seoul, to assure China that a unified Korea will be nuclear-free and be a force for peace.[58] If China can be persuaded that a renewed alliance will not be a threat, the US can achieve both regional stability and gaining a powerful ally.

Although I agree with the logic, the Chinese perception that I have researched and cited nevertheless suggest otherwise. Despite our best intentions, the burden of perception rests with Beijing. The majority of Chinese analysts express opposition against continued U.S. troops on its backdoor, a position which is easily understood if we see the region from China's eyes. Just as Washington proclaimed the Monroe Doctrine to drive European powers out of the American hemisphere, China may well want to prevent rival powers from operating in its backyard, especially when at a time when its capacity is growing.

Conclusion

The Korean peninsula has often been described as a possible contingency, a possible flashpoint of conflict between the U.S. and China. I agree wholeheartedly. The challenges are vast, especially with unification, which will require a new security regime that can sustain peace, prevent conflict, and satisfy all related parties. Nonetheless, I propose neutralization as a possible alternative that can provide an opportunity not only to promote strategic trust between the two superpowers, but also as a suitable regional order that can insulate the peninsula from great power politics that have cost millions of lives of Koreans, Chinese, and Americans alike.

Current debate on the peninsula is mostly focused on North Korea's development of nuclear and missile capacities. Although these are pressing issues, we must not forget to take the bigger context of the fundamental geopolitics of the peninsula that will, sometime or another, unravel when the two Koreas reunite.

[57] Ikenberry, G. John. "American Grand Strategy Toward East Asia and North Korea." US-China Relations and Korean Unification. Ed. Choi, Jinwook. Seoul: Korean Institute of Nation al Unification, 2012. 227.
[58] Council on Foreign Relations Independent Task Force on US Policy Toward the,Korean Peninsula. U.S. Policy Toward the Korean Peninsula. Eds. Richard Haass, et al. New York: Council on Foreign Relations, 2010, 23.

Joel
Jin-Kyu Lee

I propose that the slowly burgeoning discussions on Korean unification be widened further, with special focus on the thorny issue of security alignment. With a sustained debate and discussion among policymakers, each nation will better formulate their own positions, engage in consultations, and find a common security basis which can finally lay the foundation for enduring peace and stability on the peninsula, and further to the Asia-Pacific.

Works Cited

Bae, Ki Chan. K'oria, Tasi Saengjonŭi Kiroe Sŏda (Korea, Again on the Crossroads of Survival). Wisdom House, 2005.

Baker, Peter and Jane Perlez. "Obama's Road to Myanmar Is Paved With New Asia Intentions". They New York Times. 17 Nov 2012. Web.

Brzezinski, Zbignew. "Balancing the East, Upgrading the West: U.S. Grand Strategy in an Age of Upheaval." Foreign Affairs 91. 1 (Jan/Feb 2012): 97-104. Web.

Buckley, Chris. "China top military paper warns U.S. aims to contain rise." Reuters. 10 Jan 12.

Cha, Victor D. "The End of History: 'Neojuche Revivalism' and Korean Unification." Orbis 55.2 (2011): 290-7.

Chang, Liu. "Washington needs to take concrete steps to promote China-U.S. ties." China Daily. 4 Sep 12. Web.

"China condemns Senkaku amendment to U.S.-Japan security treaty." The Japan Times. 4 Dec 12.

"China's Economy picking up steam." China Daily. 26 Nov 2012. Web.

"China takes US return with aplomb." The Global Times. 21 Nov 2011. Web.

"Chinese president addresses diplomats' meeting in Beijing 17-20 Jul." Xinhua. 21 Jul 2009.

Choi, Jinwook, ed. Korean Unification and the Neighboring Powers. Seoul, Korea: NeulpumPlus, 2011.

Council on Foreign Relations Independent Task Force on US Policy Toward the,Korean Peninsula. U.S. Policy Toward the Korean Peninsula. Eds. Richard Haass, et al. New York: Council on Foreign Relations, 2010.

Dujarric, R. "Korea After Unification: An Opportunity to Strengthen the Korean-American Partnership." Korean Journal of Defense Analysis 12.1 (2000): 51-66. Web. 3/31/2012 9:13:59 PM.

Dujarric, Robert. Korean Unification and After : The Challenge for U.S. Strategy. Indianapolis, IN: Hudson Institute, 2000.

Harrison, Selig S. Korean Endgame : A Strategy for Reunification and U.S. Disengagement. Princeton, N.J.: Princeton University Press, 2002.

Ikenberry, G. John. "American Grand Strategy Toward East Asia and North Korea." US-China Relations and Korean Unification. Ed. Choi, Jinwook. Seoul: Korean Institute of Nation al Unification, 2012. 232-265.

Jia, Qinguo. "21-segiŭi chunggukgwa han'guk (China and Korea in the 21st

Century)." Chunggukŭi naeilŭl mutda (Question the Future of China). Ed. Moon, Jung In. Seoul: Samsung Economic Research Institute, 2010. 465-484. Print.

Gertz, Bill. "China has carrier-killer missile, U.S. admiral says." The Washington Times. December 27, 2010. Web.

Glaser, Bonnie. "Trouble in the South China Sea". National Security. Foreign Policy. Web. 17 Sep 2012.

Kang, Jong Il. "A Study on Korean Peninsula Reunification Via Permanent Neutrality." The Korean Journal of International Relations 41.1 (2001): 93-116.

Kaplan, Robert D. "The Geography of Chinese Power: How Far Can Beijing Reach on Land and at Sea?" Foreign Affairs. May/Jun 2010. Web.

Hughes, Christopher. "In Case You Missed It: China Dream". The Chinabeat. Web. 5 Apr 2012.

Kissinger, Henry. On China. New York : Penguin Press, 2011.

Koh, B. C. "[Untitled]." The American Political Science Review 75.3 (1981): pp. 832-833. Web.

Lampton, David M. "Beijing, Washington, and the Korean Peninsula". US-China Relations and Korean Unification. Ed. Choi, Jinwook. Seoul: Korean Institute of Nation al Unification, 2012. 232-265.

Lieberthal, Kenneth and Wang Jisi. "Addressing US-China Strategic Distrust". John L. Thornton China Center Monograph Series. 4 (Mar 2012).

Mead, Walter Russel. "Game of Thrones: US Pushes Naval Buildup In Asia". Via Media. The American Interest. Web. 2 Jun 2012.

Mearsheimer, John. "The Rise of China will not be Peaceful at all." The Australian. 18 Nov 05.

Moon, Chung-in. "DIPLOMACY OF DEFIANCE AND FACILITATION: THE SIX PARTY TALKS AND THE ROH MOO HYUN GOVERNMENT." Asian Perspective 32.4 (2008): 71,105,1-2.

Nathan, Andrew and Andrew Scobell. "How China Sees America." 91. (Sep/Oct 2012): 97-104. Web.

National Intelligence Council. "Global Trends 2030: Alternative Worlds." Dec 2012.

Nye, Joseph. "Should China be Contained?" CNN. Web.

Pomfret, John. "U.S. takes a tougher tone with China". The Washington Post. 30 Jul 12. Web.

Sanger, David. "Leaked Cables Depict a World Guessing About North Korea." The New York Times 29 Nov. 2010. Web.

Santis, Hughe De. "The China Threat and the "Pivot" to Asia." Current History. September 2012: 209-215.

Shambaugh, David. "Coping with a Conflicted China." Washington Quarterly. 34.1 (Winter2010/2011): 7-27.

Snyder, Scott. "Value and Significance of Korean Reunification within the Dynamics of Northeast Asia." SERI Quarterly 4.1 (2011): 41,47,6.

Swaine, Michael. "Chinese Leadership and Elite Responses to the U.S. Pacific Pivot." China Leadership Monitor. No.38.

Walt, Stephen. "Explaining Obama' s Asia Policiy." A realist in an ideological age. Foreign Policy. Web. 4/5/2012.

Wang, Fei-Ling. "Status Quo Reassessed: China's Shifting Views on Korean Unification". US-China Relations and Korean Unification. Ed. Choi, Jinwook. Seoul: Korean Institute of Nation al Unification, 2012.129-186.

Wang, Jisi. "Chunggukŭi daemi chŏngch'aek – hyŏmnyŏk vs. taehang (Chinese Policy toward the US – Cooperation v. Conflict)." Chunggukŭi naeilŭl mutda (Question the Future of China). Ed. Moon, Jung In. Seoul: Samsung Economic Research Institute, 2010. 117-144. Print.

---. "China's Search for a Grand Strategy: A Rising Great Power Finds Its Way." Foreign Affairs. 90.2 (Mar/Apr 2011): 68-79.

Yan, Xuetong. "How Assertive Should a Great Power Be?" The New York Times

---. "How China Can Defeat America." The New York Times

Yoon, Duk Min. "T'ongil, oegyoe Talryŏitta (Unification Depends on Diplomacy)." KBS T'ongil Daet'oron (Grand Discussion on Unification). KBS. 5 Aug. 2011. Discussion.

Yoon, Young Kuan. "Hanbandoŭi Miraerrŭl Malhada (The Future of the Korean Peninsula)." Sinnyŏnkihoek t'ŭkchip Daet'oron (New Year's Special Grand Discussion). KBS. 15 Jan.2011. Television. Discussion.

Zhang, Yunling. "Chunggukŭi daechŏllyakgwa asia chiyŏkjuŭi (Chinese Grand Strategy and Regionalism in Asia)." Chunggukŭi naeilŭl mutda (Question the Future of China). Ed. Moon, Jung In. Seoul: Samsung Economic Research Institute, 2010. 197-236. Print.

Zheng, Bijian. "Hwap'yŏnggulgi – Chungguk wihyŏbrongwa punggoeronŭl nŏmŏsŏ (Peaceful Rise – Beyond Theories of the Chinese Threat and the Chinese Collapse)." Chungguk ŭi naeilŭl mutda (Question the Future of China). Ed. Moon, Jung In. Seoul: Samsung Economic Research Institute, 2010. 21-40. Print.

Zhu, Feng. "Unification of Two Koreas: On View of China." Twenty Years after German Unification and Preparing for Korean Unification. Korean Institute for National Unification. Lotte Hotel, Seoul. 5 Oct. 2010. Presentation II.

Princess Maker: Between Fantasy & Reality

This paper explores various norms, values, and stereotypes tied to and reinforced by the narratives of the famous Japanese game Princess Maker. As the title implies, the player interacts with the game-world as a creator through the role of the father figure whose fairy daughters wish it is to become a human princess. Considering the longstanding mystical fascination associated with the idea of a princess, the most seemingly pertinent question to ask of the game is to reveal whether or not it perpetuates the notion that princesses are simply objects of desire. In the process, it draws upon unofficial, private game strategy guides of various netizens.

In the conclusion I find that within the larger frameworks of the game, such discussion becomes insignificant with the game's emphasis on what it means to be 'human.'

Rachel Jiyeon Lee *is a junior majoring in International Comparative Studies and Japanese at Duke. She used to play Princess Maker a lot when she was little and looks forward to playing the newer versions in her spare time.*

Princess Maker (プリンセスメーカー) is a Japanese video game series that has gained wide popularity among young girls across Asia. The third version of the series that will be discussed is also known as Princess Maker: Fairy Tales Come True. In the game, the player in his/her role as the "father," adopts and raises a fairy daughter whose only wish it seems is to simply to become a human princess.

The title of the game reflects the historical, societal fascination with the idea of princess. For example, a section of the People magazine, named "Royals," is devoted to the life of the royal family, especially that of Princess Kate in England. In particular, the "Kate's Newlywed Life" subsection provides a glimpse into the life of the picture-perfect princess on her various royal duties. Her graceful facial expressions and gestures, along with her beautiful dress and makeup, deliver the level of elegance expected by the general public, for someone holding a royal status (Mock). A New York Times article summarizes her fame and popularity succinctly with the comment "she is like an old-time Hollywood star, full of mystery, a canvas onto which the world can project its fantasies" (Lyall). Statements such as these reveal the complex of mixed interpretations surrounding princess figures: are princesses simply passive objects of patriarchal gaze and desire, or can they be representations of female empowerment?

In this paper I explore the different norms, values, and stereotypes created and reinforced by the narratives of Princess Maker, and whether these ultimately support either of the two aforementioned competing interpretations surrounding the idea of the princess. In the process, I will draw upon unofficial, private game strategy guides of various netizens in order to create a more detailed picture of the plaintiffs.

I. The Father Figure

Considering that the intended, target players of the game are pre-teen and teenage girls, it is interesting that the player assumes the role of the father. While this gender-crossing seemingly allows for players to transcend the gender boundaries, its ironic role ultimately reinforces the patriarchal ideology of the father figure as the breadwinner of the family. However, the lack of the visual image

of the father (as the game is played through the eyes of the father) and the details regarding his daily work offers another perspective on the matter. The virtual father's life is centered on raising his precious daughter, whereas the typical image of the breadwinner father is relatively detached from the daughter's life as he is too busy with work. Departing from the traditional, normative model of two parents, the noticeable absence of the mother further highlights the father's responsibility. Therefore, the devotional and emotional sensitivity required in the game on the part of the player allows for re-interpretation and re-imagination of the breadwinner role.

The role of the father determines and "brands" the daughter's fate, as the actions taken will lead to the ultimate occupation of the daughter when she reaches adulthood at the age of 18. At the very start, the father chooses with the help of the fairy guardian Uzu, the personal information for his daughter and himself, such as name, date of birth, and blood type. While seemingly trivial, the date of birth chosen actually acts to determine the nature of the relationship between the daughter and the father. For example, they will share a tighter bond if they have the same birthdays (Koeun0322). The date of birth of the daughter also determines her zodiac sign, which in turn affects her personality and her initial, monthly rise and fall in her statistics of stamina, intellect, energy, pride, morality, refinement, character, sense, charm, martial arts skill, credibility, and stress levels ("プリンセスメーカー"). To illustrate this as an example, a Scorpio daughter will be born with a relatively low morality level (" プリンセスメーカー"). In addition, the blood type of the daughter, symptomatic of Japanese fascination with blood types, is especially integral to forming the daughter's personality. For example, type A daughter will likely be more introverted, stress-vulnerable, and patient; type B daughter more outgoing, carefree, and clumsy; type AB daughter more perky and sensitive; type O daughter more confident and self-centered (Koeun0322). These personalities reflect the typical, casual associations made in the mainstream Japanese discourse for entertainment purposes (Evans).

Moreover, while the limited options of occupations of the father and the resulting life pathways are inevitably tied with the budget and technology of the production of the game, the premeditated, one-dimensional associations between the father's occupation and the daughter's personality and statistics reinforce stereotypes and overlook multiple histories and possibilities of different families across time and space. For example, the father is limited to six occupations to choose from: merchant, man of the cloth (monk),

Rachel
Jiyeon Lee

retired knight, performer, fallen noble, and bard (wanderer). Each occupation is strongly tied to the level of family income and the daughter's personality. The merchant begins with a 3000g with the annual income of 100-500g and an over-prideful, arrogant daughter; the man of the cloth with the initial 800g, the annual 700g, and a happy, friendly daughter; the retired knight with the initial 1500g, the annual 700g, and a happy, kind daughter; the performer with the initial 300g, the annual 10-800g, and a rebellious, disgruntled daughter; the fallen noble with the initial 500g, the annual 500g, and an arrogant daughter; the bard with simply the initial 5000g and a rebellious daughter (KitKat). More specifically, the type of occupations will result in different changes to be regularly made in the levels of the daughter's statistics. For example, the retired knight's daughter will experience a monthly 0.5 rise in her stamina, pride, morality, refinement, character, and martial arts skills, whereas the bard's daughter will experience a monthly -1 in her morality level and a monthly +0.5 in her stamina, energy, sense, charm, martial arts skills, and stress levels ("プリンセスメーカー"). The assumptions implicated here are that the retired knight will provide the daughter a safe, healthy, affluent environment and the bard relatively an unsafe, adventurous, challenging environment. Even though the game offers possibility for changes in the daughter's personality, her fate is still strongly tied to the family income, again emphasizing the importance of material life. For example, if the father spends above his credit limit, the daughter will immediately change into a visually worried character. But while the father daughter-relationship is largely defined materially, the game offers some room for emotional conversations to take place. The father can choose from a few model conversations for a bonding experience with the daughter: "lovingly," "gently," and "strictly." Each will consequently affect the daughter's statistics in different ways, depending on the daughter's mood (Nuriko).

II. Sense of the Self

While taking on the role of the father, a typical, young female player may closely identify with the "daughter" who is of the same gender and of a similar age. By helping and watching the daughter grow and mature, the player is able to live a virtual, alternate reality where the player has much freedom and responsibility over her projected virtual self, the daughter. In the process of self-realization, the player may gain a sense of empowerment. On the other hand, the daughter herself does not have much control over her pre-adulthood life that is largely planned by the father, who decides what she does and what she can have. Nevertheless, in response, the daughter openly and spontaneously expresses her emotions, thoughts, and desires that affect her statistics and actions. Therefore, the father figure provides her the material life, whereas the daughter actively consumes and interprets her material life. Whether the daughter has a true "free-will" or not, remains ambiguous and is subject to interpretation.

As for the daughter's material life, most visibly, the father has many items that can be purchased for the daughter, who will in response react happily, arrogantly, or as financially concerned. At a local shop, he can choose from a range of items that strengthen existing stereotypes of what young girls desire or should own: a teddy bear, poetry book, roses, food, summer dress, winter dress, casual attire, lovely gown, fancy dress, and a smile. Interestingly, the fact that a smile (0g) can be purchased demonstrates that material means are not the only way to provide happiness to the daughter. From a visiting merchant, he can choose from more expensive, diverse set of items: a dark dress, south country dress, bunny dress, fairy honey, smart fruit, apple of pride, moral's seed, noble spring water, tender comb, sugar of the arts, perfume de charm, and sword of the almighty. However, the daughter is not always on the receiving end. On the father's birthday, she will buy a gift for him, which will positively increase her various maturity levels (KitKat).

Furthermore, self-realization, on both the daughter's and the father's part, can be achieved through combination of different types of work and classes the daughter can engage in. Departing from the traditional image of the helpless, vulnerable child, the daughter is expected to work to not only supplement the family income, but also for her education, vacations, and items. Her extensive engagement with a certain work and class can lead her to become a professional in the field, even though such life path may betray her initial goal of becoming a human princess.

To illustrate, there are twelve different types of work, some of which are offered to her spontaneously: house work (1g), day care (12g), maid (12g), sales girl (12g), farm (14g), waitress (15g), tutor (16g), mason/carpentry (18g), ore miner (20g), royal maid (4g), bar hostess (25g), and bar guard (23g). Through work, she gains different life and technical skills and also learns to cope with physical and mental stress from work. For example, through day care, she will learn to appreciate the valuable relationships she builds with the children at the site, overall increasing her morals and energy/temperament. If the daughter chooses to work part-time as a bar

hostess, her refinement decreases while her charms increase. Working as a royal maid opens up the possibility for the daughter to meet the playful prince who will be in disguise. Overall, the simplified, fixed associations among the type of work, the pay rate, and the influenced statistics are unfortunately symptomatic of reality in which, for example, contribution to housework is unpaid and largely unrecognized (KitKat).

The father has multiple options for the daughter's education as well, many of which focus on improving traditionally "feminine" qualities of charm and refinement rather than rational, intellectual, physical abilities traditionally associated with masculinity: math and science (10g), fight dojo/gym (13g), dance class (13g), cooking (10g), music class (15g), art class (15g), charm school (15g), church (3g), and diet class (5g) (KitKat). Each class will influence the daughter's different statistics, with charm schools increasing refinement, for example. In classes, she also befriends her female rivals that not only bring out her competitive instinct but also helps her think about the dynamics of human relationships. Interestingly, no male characters are presented as the daughter's rival; a boy whose name is unrevealed may make an appearance and have a casual, romantic relationship with the daughter outside of school and/or church (Pmu114).

Like a real child, the daughter experiences a wide range of emotions depending on her activities, rise and fall in her statistics, and her age level. At times, she will express these thoughts and feelings through her playful or serious, philosophical conversation with Uzu, her fairy guardian, or with the father. Depending on her maturity level, her thoughts may seem naïve or in-depth. For example, if the daughter has a high level of pride, she will ponder about the idea of human pride, and say "humans need pride, because without pride they are no different from animals" to which Uzu will sadly respond "but animals like monkeys and birds, do have pride, you know. (Mumbles to herself) I hope she hasn't forgotten about her fairy times" (Koeun0322). Additionally, when she reaches a certain level of intelligence, she will express her desire to learn and say "I think I really like learning. I want to learn a lot of different things. Can this be what they call an 'intellectual appetite'? I don't think I had this kind of feeling back then as a fairy?" (Koeun0322). The daughter's reference to her fairy times allows her to compare her previous fairy life with her present human life. Such active questioning and interpretation of the self and the surrounding environment not only is a maturing process for the daughter but can also be a learning process for the player in observation. These kinds of realistic, relatable conversations may allow the players to become more emotionally attached to the game and to the daughter.

While the existence of a "true" agency of the daughter is open to debate, it is clear that "others," including the player —who, as the father, will constantly check upon her numerical statistics levels— subject her to constant observation and evaluation. The gaze of the "others" is especially visible through her participation in the annual nation-wide events: the New Year's festival, the Cherry Blossom festival, and the Harvest festival. In all three festivals, the daughter stands among a group of girls, in front of the royal family or the townspeople. With a casual glance, the competitions seem to be "fair" and "reasonable" as the winners are determined by their inner beauty represented by their statistics, rather than by their external beauty. For example, those with a high level of refinement are likely to win the New Year's festival; a high level of charm for the Cherry Blossom festival; a high level of stamina for the Harvest festival ("プリンセスメーカー"). However, the girls are inevitably objectified in the eyes of the public who will judge them with their limited, superficial understanding of the girls. In particular, the fact that the public is represented by the king or the prince who present the monetary awards, reinforces the traditional, stereotypical gender dichotomy in which women are passively subjected to the active gaze of the male.

III. The "Ending"

The ending is a culmination of the father's material, emotional devotion to the daughter. When the daughter reaches adulthood, she chooses her life path among 60 possible "endings," based on her own thoughts or on others' advice (KitKat). For example, when the daughter has taken significant amount of arts and dance classes, she will announce the father one day that she has passed the audition for the royal acting troupe, and that she wishes to become a professional actress (Koeun0322). However, such case of active job search is rare; the daughter's future is most likely be shaped by the gaze of others to which she will happily conform. To illustrate, if the daughter excels in the dance class, the dance teacher will visit home and recommend that she be a professional dancer (Koeun0322). Another example is that in some cases the prince, whether mole, cat, human, or a rabbit princess, will visit her home to propose to her (Koeun0322). In both scenarios, the daughter without second thoughts will happily accept their recommendation or proposal.

In any case, the daughter's satisfaction with her life path portrays a sense of individualism and positive outlook on life. Nevertheless, she

Rachel
Jiyeon Lee

exhibits a form of self-consciousness in her last message to the father regarding her career decision; her affectionate message ultimately reflects her desire to gain father's approval and his understanding. To exemplify, the daughter who becomes the national hero asks her father to "proudly" welcome her when she comes back home. However, her self-consciousness never leads her to question her career choice, reflecting her confidence. The daughter who becomes a concubine of the king, reflects upon her decision and says "I know it's a bit ridiculous, but I think the marriage is worth it. I will try my best to love him." Her self-consciousness and her desire to gain her father's recognition point to a sense of humanity (Koeun0322).

The ending offers a further complex picture, intertwined with various moral judgments contingent on reality. The daughter is subjected to gossip and evaluation by the townspeople and her friends regarding her career decision. Such virtual reality does not stray much from actual reality in which people are constantly identified, judged, and branded by the kind of activities or occupations they engage in. For example, the townspeople talk about the daughter's infamous involvement in a gang and sadly comment "she was so cute and fairylike when she was little" (Koeun0322) One of her friends also says "even with your extraordinary martial arts skills, a weak heart will lead you to the devil" (Koeun0322). At the very end, the daughter's fairy mother makes a solemn, ultimate statement about the daughter's life choice, and says in the case of the gang leader daughter "to be above others is a sign of a big person. But it is all meaningless if it is through illegitimate means" (Koeun0322). While such statement reveals the producers' projection of their moral standards into the game, the absence of daughter's moral questioning of her life path allows for the moral ambiguity of the game to be retained.

IV. Conclusion

Ideally, the father's goal is to fulfill the daughter's wish of becoming a human princess, as the name Princess Maker implies. However, the different life paths of 60 possible "endings," all of which the daughter is satisfied and happy with, show that the purpose of raising the daughter exists beyond the simple idea of achieving the ends. For the daughter, living the life of a princess may simply be one way of life, among many others. Therefore, whether or not the game endorses the idea of princess as an object of gaze or desire, or as a form of female empowerment, becomes rather insignificant in the larger narrative framework of the game. Ultimately, it is the

individual player who projects his or her personal desire onto the daughter, shapes her future, and evaluates personal "success" based on the outcome of the daughter's future. To borrow Ko's description of the Hello Kitty figure, the game itself is "non-contextual that it creates neither harm nor good" (Ko 182); the player who consumes the game, by actively interpreting its narratives, creates meaning out of the virtual experience.

The game, more importantly, asks the question of what it means to be "human." Through the character of the daughter who explores her newfound human identity, the game brings in many aspects of human life, especially of relationships. Beyond the materiality, the daughter's relationships with the father, co-workers, teacher, classmates, and the townspeople, are what ultimately shape the dynamics of her life. In the process, the daughter experiences growth in her maturity, as real children do in life.

Rachel
Jiyeon Lee

Works Cited

Evans, Ruth. "Japan and blood types: Does it determine personality?" BBC News. BBC News. 4 Nov. 2012. Web. 13 Dec. 2012. <http://www.bbc.co.uk/news/magazine-20170787>

KitKat. "Princess Maker 3." KitKat's Princess Maker Corner. KitKat's Princess Maker Corner. 2007. Web. 11 Dec. 2012. <http://www.kkpmc.net/pm3/pm3.htm>

Ko, Yu-Fen. "Consuming differences: 'Hello Kitty' and the identity crisis in Taiwan." Postcolonial Studies 6.2 (2003): 175-189. Print.

Koeun0322. "프린세스 메이커 3 공략 (Princess Maker 3 Strategies)." Naver. Naver. 2012. Web. 8 Dec. 2012.<http://blog.naver.com/PostList.nhn?blogId=koeun0322&from=postList&categoryNo=43>

Lyall, Sarah. "Fixating on a Future Royal as Elusive as Cinderella." The New York Times. The New York Times. 21 Apr. 2011. Web. 11 Dec. 2012.

<http://www.nytimes.com/2011/04/21/world/europe/21kate.html>

Mock, Jane. "FIRST DIAMOND JUBILEE TOUR." People. People. 27 Apr. 2012. Web. 11 Dec. 2012. <http://www.people.com/people/package/gallery/0,,20395222_20590696,00.html#21151935>

Nuriko. " Princess Maker 3: Faery Tales Come True." Nuriko's Princess Maker Nexus. Nuriko's Princess Maker Nexus. 2005. Web. 11 Dec. 2012.

<http://princessmaker.maison-otaku.net/princessmkr3.html>

Pmu114. "I love Princess Maker." Naver. Naver. 2008. Web. 8 Dec. 2012.

<http://blog.naver.com/pmu114>

"プリンセスメーカーシリーズ攻略情報まとめ (Princess Maker Series Collection of Strategies)" Wikipedia. Wikipedia. 2012. Web. 8 Dec 2012. <http://www26.atwiki.jp/princessmaker1-5/pages/32.html>

Princess Maker: Fairy Tales Come True. Gainax. V 3. 1997. Japanese.

Tibet Policy Under Deng:
A Critical Assessment of the Causes & Consequences of His Approach

From the newly rehabilitated mind of the Party veteran Deng Xiaoping sprang forth series of socio-economic reforms unprecedented in modern Chinese history. It is clear that Deng's policy of Gaigekaifang had far-reaching political and psychological effects in the Chinese periphery. Their new-found sense of pragmatism brought a momentary hope to the otherwise stark history of Sino-Tibetan dialogues. What followed were a series of exchanges that to this day remain a point of discussion and contention.

The long-standing question in the Tibetan diaspora surrounds the 1978 developments asks whether there truly was a hope for the long touted peaceful resolution, and can only be answered through a careful analysis of the partisan positions in what was often a mired dialogue. Within these two sides their remain the everpresent figures of the Chinese Communist Party (CCP) and the embodiment of the Tibetan postion, His Holiness the Dalai Lama, and it is through their positions and those of their emissaries that the consequences of Deng's policy become apparent.

Palden Gyal *was born in Tibet and grew up in India. He is currently a senior at Trinity College, Duke University, majoring in Philosophy & History with a minor in Political Science. Palden writes poems, op-eds & articles, and has published number of pieces in both print and online journals. Palden plans to pursue his further studies in the field of comparative philosophy and aspires to be both an academic philosopher and an activist for social justice and the freedom of Tibet. He keeps a philosophy blog:* http://emptinez.me/ *where he archives his short philosophical journals and enquiries. He can be reached at* paldengyal@live.no

I. Introduction

The dialogues initiated by Deng Xiaoping in December 1978 is indisputably one of the most significant developments in the recent history of Sino-Tibetan politics after establishing complete control over Tibet in 1959 by China and the Dalai Lama's flight into exile. It was a moment in history which Nehru may well have called a 'tryst with destiny' for Tibet, not for the specific terms of the negotiations, but rather due to the symbolic implications it would have had for Tibet's future political aspirations. Firstly, it was at this point in time the Sino-Tibetan conflict came closest to resolution through negotiations, as there was serious interest expressed by both parties. There are of course various strategic reasons, like the fear of a Soviet-Tibet friendship forming for example, to be taken into account on both sides as to why this had come about. Secondly, the political rapprochement had serious implications on the future trajectory of the conflict in subsequent generations of Chinese leadership. Some clear instances to analyze are the rise of hardliners in the CCP and the Dalai Lama's policy of internationalizing Tibet.

This paper begins by analyzing Deng's policy on the 'Tibetan problem' while it simultaneously scrutinizing both its underlying causes, as well as its immediate and long-term consequences on the future of the conflict. As Ezra Feivel Vogel argues in his most recent work, *Deng Xiaoping and the Transformation of China*, Deng's policy of Gaige Kaifang (改革開放), or the 'road to economic reform and openness', did not come only as a colossal change in China's domestic market and foreign policy, but through a transformation of its entire internal socio-economic structure. This had a huge impact on his policy regarding the problem of Tibet into which this paper strives to delve deep. Because Deng recognized the inevitable obstacle that both Tibet and Taiwan represented to China's ambitions to embrace the international market.

As noted above, a clear example of this was the possibility of a Soviet-Tibet friendship; a great source of concern for Deng as the relationship between two communist giants became troubled after China's rapprochement with the United States. So, along with the Four Modernizations, the "reunification" with the Taiwanese and

Tibetan exiles was clearly at the top of Deng's agenda during the Gaige Kaifang. Following the Cultural Revolution's persecutions, the Party Secretary Hu Yaobang's implemented rectificatory policy reforms in Tibet in early 80's, he turned towards the Tibetans in exile to settle the conflict by primarily proposing the return of the Dalai Lama under certain conditions like his status in relation to Tibet and the PRC. Though the Tibetan Government in Exile rejected the proposal, it expressed the desire to negotiate under certain conditions. However, there was an atmosphere of inflexibility among the politicians in Dharamsala (the seat of the Exile government) and therefore the negotiations ended in utter deadlock.

fig.1 In April 1951, Deng Xiaoping (right, front row) welcoming the Tibetan government delegation headed by Ngapoi Ngawang Jigmei (left, front row) which was on its way to Beijing for talks with the Central Government.

II. Background of the Negotiations

(a) Crossing the river by feeling the stones

The notion of regime insecurity holds that it generates incentives to compromise in territorial disputes for two reasons: Firstly, to settle and stabilize internal threats to territorial integrity that usually occur as unrest or rebellions and secondly, external cooperation is important to states whose political institution suffers from limited capacity (Fravel, 2005). Fravel explains how China has offered substantial compromises in seventeen out of twenty-three territorial disputes active since 1949. With the launching of Gaige Kaifang, Deng famously argued with an old Sichuan proverb: "It doesn't matter if a cat is black or white, so long as it catches mice", which clearly demonstrated his pragmatism and summed up the agenda of

liberalization. Therefore, it is under these contexts that one has to examine the factors leading to Deng's rapprochement with the Dalai Lama in 1978, with both the internal and external factors that contributedto his policy. Deng started with his 'reunification' program with Taiwan right after securing the post of paramount leader of the Chinese Communist Party with his loyal comrades Zhao Ziyang as the Premier in 1980 and Hu Yaobang as the Party Chairman in 1981, after carefully outmaneuvering his opponents (Evans, 1993, 252).

(b) Realism and Desparation: The Dalai Lama & his Adminstration

The active response by Dharamsala can arguably be seen as a combination of realism on the part of the Dalai Lama, and desperation amongst the exile leadership. Realism sprung from the Dalai Lama's realization that it would be better to negotiate based upon greater autonomy. Desperation, for they had no other alternative available after the signaling of the Nixon administration's abandonment of the cause by courting Beijing in early 1970's. With the dawning of the Sino-American rapprochement (Norbu, 1991, 351), the CIA suspended all military aid and connections to the Tibetan resistance movement in Mustang, Nepal in 1979. The U.S. started pulling back from Vietnam and Tibet's geopolitical significance for the U.S. was no longer a priority (Sewell, 2002, 102). Even though the Dalai Lama had no direct connection to the resistance movement, it is reasonable to assume that he had some hopes for the movement because of its secret alliance with the U.S.

The Dalai Lama argues that his approach of middle-path policy is mutually beneficial and cooperative as Tibet is for the truly autonomous Tibetan state will necessarily be dependent upon China in terms of its economic development, while China would benefit in turn from Tibet's rich spiritual traditions. In a sense, one could see this proposal as returning or restoring the old priest-patron relationship or suzerainty that was first properly established under the Mongol Yuan Dynasty, and that also arguably extended into Manchu China.

The Dalai Lama's decision to give up complete independence caused an internal fracture in the Tibetan refugee movement in exile, an essential point to which we will revisit later in this paper It suffices to say that the Dalai Lama and the Tibetan exile leadership invested far too much political economy and had naively high hopes in the tacit olive branch offered by the post-Gaige Kaifang PRC. Their

optimism stemmed from their simplistic and naïve interpretation of the difference heralded by the inauguration of Deng Xiaoping in the Communist party. Yet his approach to solving the problem of Taiwan, his open door policy to the international community, and Hu Yaobang's substantial reforms in Tibet in early 80's understandably exhibited an immense potential for future reforms that China was going through were the reasons for the Dalai Lama's optimism.

III. Bargaining and Boundaries of the Negotiation

On December 3, 1978, through the Dalai Lama's elder brother, Gyalo Dhondup, Deng conveyed his three summative points on the Tibetan problem, as Dawa Norbu puts them: first, "…so long as the premise that Tibet is a part of China is not accepted, there is nothing to talk about…" , which the Tibetan's interpreted as, 'anything except independence'. Second, Deng urged the Dalai team to come and investigate actual conditions in Tibet, which could be done through 'fact-finding delegations' for a number of times before and after the two formal talks. Third and lastly, he accepted the Tibetan suggestion to send fifty Tibetan teachers from India to teach in various parts of Tibet (Norbu, 1991, 353). This then would form the preparatory phase of the negotiations that would take place in Beijing after four years.

After having made what he would have considered were the necessary economic concessions and reparatory establishments in Tibet, Hu Yaobang specified Party line on various issues including the Dalai Lama's personal status upon his return to China. On July 28, 1981, Gyalo Dhondup secretly met with Hu Yaobang in Beijing, during which Hu articulated his five-points on which the rapprochement with the Dalai Lama would be built:

1. The Dalai Lama should be confident that China has entered a new stage of long term political stability, steady economic growth and mutual help among all nationalities.

2. The Dalai Lama and his representatives should be frank and sincere with the Central Government, and not beat around the bush. There should be no more quibbling over the events in 1959.

3. The central authorities sincerely welcome the Dalai Lama and his followers to come back to live. This is based on the hope that they will contribute to upholding China's unity and promoting solidarity between the Han and Tibetan nationalities, and among all nationalities, and the modernization program.

4. The Dalai Lama will enjoy the same political status and living conditions as he had before 1959. It is suggested that he shall not go to live in Tibet or hold local posts there. Of course, he may go back to Tibet from time to time. His followers need not worry about their jobs and living conditions. These will only be better than before.

5. When the Dalai Lama wishes to come back, he can issue a brief statement to the press. It is up to him to decide what he would like to say in the statement (Goldstein, 1997, 68).

fig.2 In 1979 when Gyalo Thondup, the Dalai Lama's brother met Deng Xiaoping, the Chinese Paramount Leader

He must have presumed that given the substantial changes in Tibet, the Dalai Lama would have felt gratitude, yet in this sense he was as far from comprehending Dharamsala's true political aspirations as possible (Rabgey & Sharlho, 2004). So it was that the Dalai Lama's reaction to the Chinese five-point proposal was curt and clear: "Instead of addressing the real issues facing six million Tibetan people, China has attempted to reduce the question of Tibet to a discussion of my own personal status" (Norbu, 1991, 354). From this exchange it is clear that Hu's five-point policy's primary interest in negotiations was to persuade the Dalai Lama to return "home". Reading the specific conditions under which the Dalai Lama could return, one can assume that Hu and the PRC went into negotiations expecting the Dalai Lama's acceptance. Yet the simple reductionism of the Tibetan issue down to the Dalai Lama's personal matters revealed their supposition of the Dalai Lama as the sole architect of China's Tibet problem. By now it should be clear that a deep misunderstanding of the conflict by the PRC as how Tibetans conceived it (Rabgey & Sharlho, 2004), as well as how they

in turn perceived the PRCs remonstrations. And thus it was that the negotiations, seemingly doomed from the start, broke down.

Nevertheless, in 1982, there was still some interest within PRC leadership in continuing the call for Dalai Lama's return, but this time on more narrowly defined terms and to hold formal talks in Beijing with the representatives of the Dalai Lama (Rabgey & Sharlho, 2004, 7). Even though the Tibetans were disappointed with Hu Yaobang's proposal, given that it reduced the scope of the discussion, the overwhelmingly positive reception to the representatives and with Deng's initial assurance that "all matters can be discussed with the only negation of independence", their hopes for the negotiations remain strong. As a result, despite the fact that the discussion blueprint was Hu's five-point policy, the delegates put forward the Dalai Lama's vision for the political future of Tibet. They demanded the incorporation of all Tibetan-inhabited areas under a single administrative unit whose political structure would be democratic (Rabgey & Sharlho, 2004). The Tibetan delegates also argued for a higher degree of autonomy than that offered to Taiwan based on its historically non-Chinese ethnicity and unique cultural and religious traditions (Smith, 2003). The response from the PRC was curt: "Tibet has been liberated for more than three decades and it has been under the leadership of the Central government since…the nine-point principle (offered to Taiwan), therefore, is not applicable to Tibet (Smith, 2003, 63)." Beijing would brook no mention of Tibet's political status with the sole exception of the Dalai Lama's return policy. The Chinese were confident that the Tibetans would be happy under the PRC assured since there had been no significant protest of Communist rule in Tibet since the 1959 event. The Tibet's historical, ethic and cultural distinctiveness caused no grief on the conscience of the PRC negotiators, for them Tibet was merely an incorporated entity within the fifty-six ethnic nationalities.

Though there was no substantive consequence from the previous talk, the end of October 1984 saw the same three delegates of Tibetan exile government sent to Beijing for discussions. This time, the PRC officials set had reduced the defined parameters for the discussion down to nothing less than unconditional return of the Dalai Lama (Smith, 2003, 63). They furthermore rebuked the Tibetans for the deceitful actions of the Dalai Lama, who spoke of improving relations while his followers carry on advocating Tibetan independence. The Chinese had a reason to doubt the Dalai Lama as the Tibetan movement for its cause has split into two main factions. The exile government led by the Dalai Lama for "greater

Palden
Gyal

autonomy" and the Tibetan Youth Congress (TYC) along with small youth groups advocating complete independence (Davis, 2009, 157). Therefore, there was no ground for any negotiations under those conditions. Soon after the meeting, Hu Yaobang's Tibet policy came under criticism within the PRC by the hardliners for reviving Tibetan religion and nationalism (Davis, 157).

IV. Talk or Tourism

As result of Chinese intransigence about the dialogue on anything but the status of the Dalai Lama, the exile government changed its strategy by drawing on international support. In January 1987, Hu Yaobang, the architect of liberalization policy in Tibet, was purged due to his radical liberalism; attacked by the hardliners who blamed him for the failure to handle the students' protest in 1986 in China and his policies on the Tibet problem (Lieberthal, 2004, 143). Subsequently, on September 21, 1987, the Dalai Lama addressed the US Congressional Human Rights Caucus, announced that he was compelled to appeal to the international community because of China's refusal to negotiate (Rabgey & Sharlho, 2004, 9). He then proposed his five-point peace plan for Tibet:

1. Transformation of the whole of Tibet into a zone of peace;

2. Abandonment of China's population transfer policy;

3. Respect for the Tibetan people's fundamental human rights and democratic freedoms;

4. Restoration and protection of Tibet's natural environment and the abandonment of China's use of Tibet for the production of nuclear weapons and the dumping of nuclear waste;

5. Commencement of earnest negotiations on the future status of Tibet and on relations between the Tibetan and Chinese peoples (Shakya, 1999, 414).

The Chinese rejected the Dalai Lama's proposal immediately, because they had already foreseen the discussion as pointless as they were a recapitulation of the terms presented by the exile representatives in the two formal talks. In hindsight it is clear that the emphasis on the idea of a "Greater Tibet" was unacceptable to the Chinese, who had previously incorporated Tibetan regions beyond the Tibet Autonomous Region (TAR). Indeed, even before 1950's most of these areas had been ruled by warlords with whom the Tibetan government in Lhasa had no direct political affiliations (Norbu, 1991). Furthermore, the condition for "demilitarization"

was another insurmountable barrier for the PRC to comply with. Tibet borders with five countries including the PRC's beleaguered neighbor, India, and therefore, it represents a region of significant strategic and geopolitical importance, and a cornerstone for the long term national security of China.

Following the Dalai Lama's address, eight Senators wrote a joint letter addressed to Zhao Ziyang (who had by then replaced Hu Yaobang), urging China to accept the Dalai Lama's proposals for negotiations (Shakya, 1999, 415). But if anything, this probably dashed any hope for negotiations, yet while all this was happening, another huge event took place in Lhasa when twenty-one monks staged a pro-independence demonstration. The Chinese response was harsh as they suppressed the uprising by beating and arresting all those involved, eerily reminiscent of the crackdown in 1959. Tibet remained under martial law for fourteen months under its new party boss Hu Jintao (Shakya, 1999). Again on June 15, 1988, the Dalai Lama addressed the European Parliament in Strasbourg in which he argued for a "self-governing democratic political entity … in association with the People's Republic of China (Rabgey & Sharlho, 2004, 11)", this proposal publicly announced that the exile government would no longer be seeking independence. This abrupt declaration came as shock and even disappointment for many Tibetans in exile, and colors disputes to this very day.

Fig.2 1997, the first Tibetan fact-finding delegation with the 10th Panchen Lama in China.

The international community received the proposal positively, but regardless of this international support, the Chinese leadership rejected it categorically. In a letter presented by the Chinese Embassy in India, New Delhi on September 23, 1988, they welcome the Dalai Lama to talks yet "clarified" two points (Rabgey & Sharlho, 2004, 12):

1. We have never recognized the "Kashag Government" which has

all along indulged in activities for independence of Tibet. We will not receive any delegation or fact-finding group designated by the Kashag government.

2. "...the new proposal by Dalai Lama cannot be the basis for the talks... it has not yet relinquished the concept of Tibetan independence."

The Tibetan reply to this was rather strong without conforming to rules (e.g. not allowed to involve any foreigners, but Tibetans included a Dutch lawyer) laid down by the Chinese to pursue the talk. The Chinese side was enraged by this violation of the procedural conditions, and criticized the Dalai Lama as "insincere" (Norbu, 1991, 361). Meanwhile, on March 7, 1989, China imposed martial law in Tibet and the Dalai Lama cut off all contacts with China. When subsequently the Tiananmen Square student's protest took place and the crackdown happened, the Dalai Lama joined the international community to condemn China despite expressing his interest in continuing the negotiation (Norbu, 1991, 362). Negotiations broke down and have never reached the same levels ever since.

Works Cited

Goldstein, Melvyn C.,1997 The Snow Lion and the Dragon: China, Tibet and the Dalai Lama, University of California Press, Los Angeles.

Evans, Richard, 1993 Deng Xiaoping and the Making of Modern China, Viking, New York.

Lieberthal, Kenneth, 2004 Governing China: from Revolution through Reform, Norton & Company, New York.

Shakya, Tsering, 1999 The Dragon in the Land of Snows: a history of modern Tibet since 1947, Penguin Compass, New York.

Mike Sewell, 2002 The Cold War, Cambridge University Press, U.K.

Davis, Elizabeth Van Wie Tibetan separatism in China, The Korean Journal of Defense Analysis, Vol. 21, No. 2, June 2009, 155-170.

Norbu, Dawa, China's Dialogues With the Dalai Lama 1979-90: Prenegotiation Stage of Dead End? Pacific Affairs, Vol. 64, No. 3 (Autumn, 1991), pp. 351-372.

Rabgey, Tashi & Sharlho, Tseten Wangchuk, Sino-Tibetan Dialogue in the Post-Mao Era: Lessons and Prospects, Policy Studies 12, East-West Center Washington, 2004.

Lixiong, Wang, Reflections on Tibet, New Left Review, Vol. 14, March-April 2002, pp.79-111.

Shakya, Tsering, Blood in the Snow: Reply to Wang Lixiong, New Left Review, Vol. 14, May-June 2002, pp.39-61.

Warren, W. Smith. Sino-Tibetan Dialogue: talk or tourism? World Tibet Network News, June 23, 2003.

Palden
Gyal

After Tiananmen:
The Human Legacy of a
Moment in History

Early in the summer of 1989, students and workers across China converged on Beijing's Tiananmen square to stage protests against China's central government. While the claims of the protesters were many, the general ethos was for democratic governance and greater government transparency. On June 4, in what has now come to be known as the infamous "Tiananmen Massacre", China's central government sent in troops to violently and quite often fatally quell dissent and disperse protesters. Thousands more were arrested or exiled in the aftermath of the protests, including the four dissidents interviewed for this piece.

Unlike existing historical accounts that chronologically detail the aftermath of the Tiananmen protests, this piece attempts to involve and resolve the individual stories of Tiananmen's veterans. Rather than focus on facts, this piece emphasizes the narrative power of their oral histories and the reverberations the year 1989 still has in the historical memory of the Chinese diaspora today.

Emily Feng is currently a Junior at Duke University, majoring in Public Policy with a minor in Chinese. She is interested in issues surrounding urbanization and development in China. At Duke, Emily writes for several publications and is a member of the Duke East Asia Nexus, serving as its co-director for the Duke-UNC China Leadership Summit, an annual conference on US-China relations.

On June 4, 1989, the Chinese Communist government violently dissolved a fifty-six-day student-led protest in Tiananmen Square, Beijing. In the massacre's aftermath, thousands of students and intellectuals fled the country, many to the United States. More than twenty years later, Chinese exiles share their individual and often discordant memories of Tiananmen...

Setting the Scene...

A festive, carnival-like atmosphere pervades the square. The hunger strikes, which at their height involved over a hundred thousand students, have been going on for more than a month. Groups of dedicated carers come and go from the square carrying water and supplies provided by sympathetic Beijing residents. Hundreds of thousands of Beijing citizens, students and workers are drawn to the square, which by now resembles a colorful tent-city, by its charged and optimistic atmosphere of protests.

> "We truly believed that we could change the Chinese government. We loved our country and we wanted to make it better, never thinking that it would ever turn on us," remembers Hui Cui, a student at Peking University in Beijing at the time and a protest participant.

The 1989 Tiananmen Square protests still stand out among all the events of the 20th century. Images from the protests, most notably that of the lone, heroic "Tank Man," bravely facing down David and Goliath style a line of army tanks, have risen sky high level of iconic cultural significance. Even for those born after the events of 1989, the image is somehow universally understood as an emblem of fragile yet powerful human defiance against the instruments of oppression, of democracy against authoritarianism. One cannot talk about the 20th century without talking about China, and one cannot talk about China without talking about Tiananmen. Indeed, the singular phrase, "Tiananmen" is enough to signify that one means the Tiananmen Square protests of 1989; a name with origins several hundreds of years old is now a linguistic shortcut to events that transpired only 24 years ago.

Only 24 years – and yet, Tiananmen has already begun to petrify in its historical amber. Untold numbers lost their lives – sometimes inadvertently so – during the protests. But what of the individuals who escaped? A lucky number emigrated or were smuggled out of the country to Europe and the United States. A bittersweet ending to a tragic story perhaps, but history never has a neat and tidy ending, for just as Tiananmen's legacy still has enduring political consequences, its key figures have dispersed all over the globe, like fallen petals blown far by the wayward breeze of vicissitudes, carrying with them the lasting and fragmented historical memory of Tiananmen Square.

Act I: Exodus

They left China in the tens of thousands. Intellectuals, artists, protesters, students and other citizens: anyone who no longer felt they had a future in China sought refuge elsewhere. In response to the persecution of student participants, several Western nations including the United States, Australia, Britain and the current countries of European Union extended visas or relaxed visa application procedures for Chinese students. The friendlier immigration policy further encouraged a sudden influx of intellectuals and students who made the United States, in particular, their new home. Surveys measuring enrollment of Chinese students in American universities show that numbers ballooned from just under 14,000 in 1986 to nearly 34,000 by 1990. By the end of the second millennium, the number of Chinese students studying at American universities, predominantly as graduate students, peaked at 54,000 with numbers continuing to rise in the years after.

A number of top American universities made themselves particularly hospitable towards the waves of Chinese academic elites who were now making their way to the United States with considerable haste. Most prominently among these universities was Princeton University which, with a generous private donation, established the highly exclusive Princeton China Initiative, an academic think tank of sorts, with all the trappings of a good, secret society of sorts. A select number of exiles were smuggled out on the wings of Operation Yellow Bird, a covert initiative that reads like it was ripped from the pages of some conspiratorial spy novel. Funded by Hong Kong business contributions and carried out by smugglers working with the Asian mafia, the Triads, Operation Yellow Bird was able to locate and extract around 40 wanted Tiananmen protesters. To this day, the complete list of dissidents who were successfully whisked out of China has never been released due to fears of reprisal.

Emily
Feng

Through means clandestine or institutionalized and whether by chance or intention, a large number of Tiananmen exiles, whose numbers sporadically grow as dissidents complete their prison terms in China, have begun a new life in the United States. Among the exile community, the memory and narrative of Tiananmen have been alternately blurred by time or refocused from new perspectives, retouched to cover uncomfortable facts or newly reinterpreted by more than two decades of reflection. Now, 24 years later, understanding the collective historical memory and legacy of Tiananmen is becoming more and more difficult. I sat down with four such members of the exile community.

Act II: Voices
Su Wei, Professor of Chinese at Yale University

Su Wei, regardless of whether he's speaking in Chinese or English, is boyishly enthusiastic and extremely loquacious. Although his combover may show signs of thinning and the years have added their commensurate weight to his figure, I can still glimpse the same kind of spunk and vitality that emanates from a picture taken of him in his early twenties, while he was still laboring on Hainan Island as one of Mao's "sent down youth" during the Cultural Revolution. Wary of being unintentionally blunt and thus insensitive, I ask him if there is anything he particularly wants to say.

He bombastically pushes my concerns aside. "My story I can tell the whole day, whole night! Doesn't matter!" "For me, anything for me I can talk. Only how to escape from China, who helped me I won't tell anyone," he adds, with a twinkle in his eye.

Like most of the older intellectuals and professors who took part in the protest, Su's unpleasant interactions with the Chinese Communist Party did not begin with Tiananmen, 1989. As the son of well-known intellectual in Guangzhou before the Cultural Revolution, Su got his first taste of being a political outsider. When his call came in 1968, he was almost relieved to leave and work in the countryside.

He returned ten, long years later when he was 25. During his time on Hainan Island, he experienced several instances of incredible human kindness, developing relationships he still cherishes to this day. When he thinks about the China that he loves, the China he misses and the China on whose behalf he joined the protests in 1989, he thinks of these ordinary Chinese people and the simple human kindness he enjoyed while in their company. After he returned, he managed to secure a place at UCLA, one of the first students from PRC to study abroad. Upon hearing of the commotion happening on the other side of the Pacific in his homeland, Su returned to China in 1986, becoming a leading intellectual in the protests. He quickly left after June 4, having been informed that he would be one of the government's biggest targets after the protests. For a while, he taught as part of the selective Princeton China Initiative before moving to Yale in 1998.

Unlike the majority of Tiananmen's participants, I felt Su hasn't tried to separate the present from the past, instead he continuously uses the first half of his life to inform the latter half. A lifelong writer, Su memorialized his long years as a reformed laborer in a poem that was eventually set to music written by Tony Fok, a fellow worker Su met on Hainan Island all those years ago. Su describes the piece, called *"Ask the Sky and the Earth: A Cantata for the Sent-down Youth,"* as a "love song" to this romanticized notion of China and its humble, warm-hearted people. He's no longer politically active however, because he stresses he "was never a politician" but instead a writer at heart. "Only I felt free to step forward. I didn't have Party connections, I wasn't married, and my parents were in Hong Kong," he recounts. He was well-educated, well-connected, well-spoken; *when history calls, you answer.* The circumstances of the time had pushed him – literally pushed to the front by friends who found him an apt spokesperson for the movement – to be something he wasn't.

Wang Juntao, New Jersey scholar

Wang Juntao is severe, clipped and direct, his speech the opposite of Su Wei's enthused verbiage. He immediately requests speaking in Chinese, recounting the facts of his hard, embattled existence with the detached matter-of-factness of the consummate survivor. "I still think about Tiananmen, but only because other people can't seem to get over it," he gruffly replies. Tiananmen was not, by any means, the worst atrocity the Chinese Communist party had perpetuated, he explains. The numbers persecuted or killed in the Cultural Revolution, the millions who starved during the Great Leap Forward; these people he can never forget and for whom he will spend his whole life remembering.

Wang is not given to sentimentalism, nor can he afford to. "When I was 17, I chose this life for myself. I could do anything – write, do politics, teach – but I chose to this way for myself." Dissent, in other words, is a way of life for Wang. Soon after he quietly made his

decision to dissent, he was arrested and jailed for 224 nightmarish days for taking part in the Tiananmen Incident of 1976, a demonstration that bears a tragic similarity to Tiananmen 1989. Sparked by the death of Zhou Enlai, a former Chinese premier who attempted to reign in the Red Guards during the Cultural Revolution, the protest used the pretense of mourning Zhou's passing to criticize China's central leaders who immediately quashed the demonstration overnight. "My prison experience when I was 17 years old was much worse than the three and a half years I spent after Tiananmen in jail," Wang remembers.

"My mother would visit me [in jail] and every time she would cry. If I wasn't mentally and emotionally tough I wouldn't have survived." Regret and guilt are things he doesn't think about because they are unproductive attitudes to have. He never has been scared of "jail, beheadings, things of that sort," he says with a laugh. Instead, politics was the most important thing he could get involved in, because politics influences every aspect of one's life, regardless of whether you pay any attention to it. Reading Wang's resume is akin to reading a history of Chinese social protest since 1976. He founded the Chinese Democracy Party, writes extensively as an academic on Chinese politics and has organized several publications and think tanks dedicated to discussing legal, political and social reform. As a student organizer during Tiananmen 1989, he organized a roundtable for representatives from all activist groups and briefly edited the well-known dissident magazine, *Beijing Spring*.

After June 4, he escaped Beijing and hid in the mountains of Hebei province where he was supposed to be picked up by operatives from Operation Yellow Bird; when plans went awry and the go-between was caught, Wang was sentenced to 13 years in jail. He fulfilled three and a half those before finally being released and sent to the U.S. in 1994 for "medical reasons" as he had contracted hepatitis B. And though he did not know it at the time, Wang was now an exile.

"Do you have anything else to ask on this matter?" he as asks, after rattling after this perfunctory summary of his tribulations, all delivered in a flat, steady stream of monotone Chinese. It's a little underwhelming, to hear him this detached account of what many would consider a rather traumatizing history of political activism. But for Wang, his work is all he can remember, what's past is past, and what has to be done moving forward is as obvious to Wang as night and day. Exile doesn't seem to particularly bother him and his geographical location doesn't really matter to him – "and anywhere is better than jail" he deadpans – because his heart will always be with the Chinese democracy movement.

"I'm at the frontier, where nothing is defined to create an alternate vision for China when the Communist regime falls," he states with the calm, brutal efficiency of a man possessed by the unshakeable belief that one day his efforts will be validated.

Li Jinjin, Immigration Lawyer – NYC

Li Jinjin feels like he was cut from the same cloth as Wang Juntao. Like Wang, he has a standardized spiel prepared for the the dwindling numbers of questioners that come his way, asking about his experiences in Tiananmen 1989. And like all the others I spoke to, Li's narrative begins long before Tiananmen. Growing up in the midst of the Cultural Revolution meant that he never received a proper day of schooling due to constant interruption of classes by struggle sessions, parades and group volunteer work; his later confinement he took as the opportunity to ceaselessly read and study that he had been denied in his earlier years.

When the protests began in April, Li was a graduate student in Constitutional Law in a doctoral program, and although he had been cautioned against becoming involved in dissent movements after getting into some trouble as a graduate student, Li quickly ascended student ranks to lead a successful sit-in on the steps of the Great Hall of People. He eventually was able to present the students' Seven Point Petition to People's Congress representatives, and after a brief hiatus from the protests, began delivering spontaneous street speeches, where he chanced upon a group of workers. After becoming the group's self-appointed legal counsel, Li joined forces with Hang Dongfang (now a Hong Kong labor activist) and Zhou Yongjun (previously exiled to the US, Zhou's whereabouts are unknown after being arrested for reentering China in 2009) among others to establish the Workers Autonomous Federation, China's first independent labor union of sorts.

Li is still unapologetic for his involvement, though he was shortly arrested after June 4 and jailed for nearly two years without a formal indictment before being released under international pressure. "I was personally very interested in trying to help China. I believe China has no freedom, no democracy. There are two laws; one on the book and the other is personal dictatorship. That is why my belief, that's why I easily got involved," he recounts. Now he works as an immigration lawyer in New York City, where he now helps recent Chinese immigrants obtain living and working permission in the US. Like Wang, Li is governed by a pragmatic, survivor's instinct. "I'm a very obstinate person with life; it's easy for me to make any adjustment

of status," he observed. When he was forced to work as a waiter to support his family through Columbia law school, he swallowed his pride and soldiered on with single-minded determination. Still today, Li holds unwaveringly to his belief in a democratic China, though his rhetoric falls along well-worn phrases and narrative structures; our conversation is peppered with buzzwords like "democracy" and "reform," but the exercise highlights just how difficult it is to talk about complex historical and cultural events without falling back on standardized retellings.

The China he sees today is disappointing, its paternalistic leadership riddled with corruption and its citizens bought off by the safe temptation of new riches. Still, he believes individual activism has its place and Li routinely speaks publicly and publishes extensively on Chinese legal and political reform. And despite the fact that he cannot go back to China, he feels at home wherever he can be free. After a brief moment to ponder his situation, he concludes, as if to himself, "I enjoy freedom. I...very like."

Kang Zhengguo,
Professor of Chinese at Yale University (retired)

Like most of the other Tiananmen exiles, Kang Zhengguo insists on speaking in Chinese, even on my part, a request I haltingly comply with. Despite having lived in the United States since 1994, Kang still lives very much in his own, self-created version, of China. His walls are tastefully decorated with Chinese art; in the middle of our conversation his wife brings me a small plate of Chinese candies from their native province of Xi'an; he admits that he almost never speaks English as he is lucky enough to teach on his twin loves, Chinese language and culture. Kang has aged into a gentle, scholarly giant of sorts, though he still looks very much like how he does in wonderful picture taken right after his first struggle session, in which his classmates and teachers denounce him for his counterrevolutionary ways. His pose is casual, hair charmingly ruffled, his eyes crinkled in a mischievous, devil may care grin.

This quietly rebellious personality earned Kang his first run in with the political powers that be, when he was expelled from college for writing politically incorrect letters to a friend. His family, deemed landlords, had already been torn apart by the Cultural Revolution. From there, he worked as a confined laborer in a Xi'an brickyard where, bored by the company of his fellow

inmates and depressed by the harsh conditions of the labor camp, he sent a mail request for a banned Russian novel. This earned him a three year prison sentence. Afterwards, he briefly lived in an agricultural commune during which he was able to shed his old identity by being adopted by an old peasant. He was teaching at Xi'an Jiaotong University when the Tiananmen protests broke out; the old rebellious spirit in him compelled him to join the angry crowds, wearing a sign reading "Point Your Guns Here" that his wife helped pin onto his shirt.

Kang was thankfully spared the worst of punishment and allowed to continue his teaching, but he was told by his superiors that he would never be promoted or experience a salary raise as a result of his party disloyalty. Kang struggled to support his family in cramped, meager quarters until finally receiving the unprecedented offer to teach Chinese at Yale University.

"June 4 threw a shadow on my life; coming here was a kind of surrender, a surrender that I couldn't remain in China. If I stayed there I would have probably continued to suffer...Even if I had been given a janitor's position, I would have wanted to do it because the environment is freer, I could learn without fear." Ever appreciative of his life circumstances, Kang loves sharing his experiences and is delighted to hear of my other contacts. "Wang Juntao and Li Jinjin! Both are my good friends," he exclaims approvingly. "Both are good people, very good people." But unlike his two friends, the mellow Kang no longer believes in activism or protest.

Instead, Kang Zhengguo is the archetypal thinker; he lives as much as much in the past as he does in the present and as much in the real, physical world as he does inside the imaginings of his own mind. Kang has made it his job to not only remember but better understand China's volatile political history and his own experience within that history. Just as dissent is a way of life for Wang Juntao, reflection and reaction are Kang's lifeblood. Originally in emulation of his paternal grandfather, Kang keeps a long series of personal diaries. His lifelong effort of recollection and meditation culminated in 2005 when he published his (now translated) memoir, *Confessions of an Innocent Life in Communist China*, with the intention to not only preserve his own memories but to also capture the absurdist historical *zeitgeist* of his generation.

"Things were extremely ridiculous and absurd. Only through writing the absurdity in these events can we capture the truth. I have

this ability to describe everyday happenings and events and capture their *sense* for fact, reality and truth are different. Truth is more abstract. Our reality has to be represented...you cannot capture truth because your memories aren't a videotape, that tape 24/7, capturing every action...So we have to reconstruct. You have to use literary techniques to do this...but this doesn't mean it's fiction....You are the narrator and the author; you have to stand outside of your own perspective, to transcend yourself and make yourself an object for study to reconstruct reality. Everyone has their memories but it's not everyone who can write a memoir."

Act III Searching for a story

And there is perhaps no one who can tell the story of Tiananmen. In the course of interviewing four participants of Tiananmen, I watched my original goals for this piece fade slowly away with every word they said. I was not going to find a definitive account of Tiananmen's cultural and psychological legacy, nor was there an account that existed for me to find that could fit together all the divergent experiences of its actors, who came from all walks of life. Part of the impossibility of generalization is unique to the social phenomenon of Tiananmen, in which people from all walks of life – students, teachers, Beijing citizens and blue collar workers – fervently supported change. Even among the selective group of people who were viciously persecuted for their involvement, there is considerable variance. The flamboyant antics of Wu'er Kaixi, a Uigher student organizer known for his brazen outspokenness during the protest and who achieved near-celebrity status shortly after his escape from China, are hardly comparable to the scholarly likes of Kang Zhengguo, for example. The only similarity between them is that they left China for their actions in Tiananmen.

Much of the impossibility of obtaining authoritative narratives is inherent in the nature of the work, however. "You are doing an interview work; you interview 100 people and from 90 people you might not gain what you wanted to gain," the same Kang preemptively pointed out to me at the beginning of our interview. "The narrator is not always a very clear narrator because a person's consciousness always is influenced by concepts, experiences and ideas. It's not that they are lying, but...when they are explaining their opinions, it is filtered."

Penetrating these filters – the hazy webs of clouded memory and the distance, historical, cultural and psychological, between interviewer and interviewee – is difficult. "Where were you born?" asks Li Jinjin rather brusquely before we begin talking. I answered the United States, quick to hedge that I had been "raised Chinese" and could speak to Chinese if he so wished. But the damage had been done; I was an outsider, someone born both outside of the temporal and cultural space in which Li belonged, and he altered his narrative accordingly to what he thought would best suit my perceived interests.

Wang Juntao, perhaps the most battle-seasoned veteran out of all of them, laughed with the slightest shadow of contempt at my naivete: "Your questions, they are all from a warm, cozy domestic perspective, questions little boys and girls would ask." He could give me the fluffy kind of stuff if I so wished, he conceded, but he was also underscoring the distinct psychosocial spaces we inhabited, spaces that were unbridgeable by a simple interview.

Language, as much as shared experience, was an equally important filter. Indeed, many of Tiananmen's most visible survivors today have continued to remain connected with their motherland through language as writers, poets and teachers of Chinese language. Those that chose to respond in Chinese – the language of the protests and the language of their culture – responded more easily, with much more force of emotion. Translation of these comments sacrificed some of this intangible quality for the sake of conciseness. Similarly, those that chose to speak in English used the same hackneyed language English narratives of Tiananmen frequently use. It's no wonder that depicting Tiananmen's legacy has been so elusive, when the act of communication and translation is prone to the standardization of uniquely individual experiences. As Perry Link, a Princeton professor at the time, later observed about the protests: "original memory impressions are always more ragged and unorganized than the stories that we tell. Putting things into words or pictures, or into rows in museums, inevitably simplifies them, smoothes them out."

In Akira Kurosawa's 1950 masterpiece *Rashomon*, four witnesses are asked to describe the circumstances surrounding the murder of a samurai and the rape of his wife, but all four accounts somehow materially contradict one another, a clever commentary on the subjectivity of reality. The same challenges apply when talking about Tiananmen. A US-educated writer, a Chinese language instructor, an immigration lawyer and a political activist: the eclectic list of

Emily
Feng

people I spoke to represent only a slice of the collective Tiananmen diaspora and the diverse opinions its members hold, and yet, if we look hard enough, we can begin to the see the faint outlines of picture emerging. The picture is complex and it isn't always clear, but it's a valuable picture nonetheless of a turning point in Chinese history.

ACT IV Calling All Protestors

Hui Cui remembers the excitement and fervor that animated campus during the protests. Hui was sitting in the cafeteria one day when she remembers, "people came in and said they were marching to the square [after the death of Hu Yaobang]; I joined in and we marched through the night before reaching the square." Copycat protests popped up on all major college campuses and urban centers, and many students travelled from other cities to Beijing to take part in the protests. Having been fed images and text that romanticized revolution and self-sacrifice, the students saw themselves as the natural successors of a long history of intellectual protest, a history of protest that had iterated itself several times before in the very square that had been co- opted by the Communist Party.

"We all believed we were fighting for a higher cause," wrote Rowena He, who is currently a Harvard professor and teaches on Tiananmen but was a Beijing resident during the time, in a recent editorial. "And we were taught that it was good to die for something more important than ourselves." Nothing to fear and nothing to lose: it was the young college student's wet dream, a chance to exercise the latent applications of an elite education, a long-awaited opportunity to cast aside theory for action.

"Nostalgia – that's a good word," Li Jinjin chuckles. Petty crime, he recounted, decreased dramatically in the days of the protests; even the criminals respected that something larger than any individual was at stake here. "People treat us like heroes, give us these thumbs. People were support us. It was a great time, for me," he remembers wistfully. "It was a movement. Almost 99% of people supported student and in that moment everyone had no fear. Everyone had no fear! But now it's different. Also, the people right now have the chance to get money through the corruption, so that's changed," he sighs.

The urgency of the those months, the huge swell of momentum that brought together students, workers and citizens together in arrangements for better or worse created some unlikely heroes. Explaining why one chooses to join political protests and throw self-preservation to the winds is hard even for the protesters themselves.

Kang "just decided" to strap on a sign and join the protests; Wang Juntao somehow decided at the age of seventeen to devote his life to protest; Li Jinjin organized a sit-in his first day in Bejing, despite being previously warned against participating; Su Wei simply returned to China and began organizing salons for leading protest intellectuals. Their experiences are corroborated by the testimonies of other Tiananmen participants. Han Dongfang, a Beijing railway worker, who went onto co-found the Beijing Autonomous Workers' Federation, a workers' union. He once remarked in an interview, "Although I never encountered the kinds of things that were starting to go on there, I immediately knew that they were important. What people were saying about there being no rights in China and about how the country would never develop without political change was exactly what was in my own heart!"

That they would immediately take part in the largest protests modern China had ever seen was a no-brainer. Some of us are born with the rebellious spark in us, a virus that lies dormant until summoned by the call of history, compelling us to step up and assume leadership and responsibility. In another world, these students and intellectuals might have lived quiet, unremarkable lives as professors, railway workers or poets. "I am not a politician; I am a writer. I was doing something I'm not," Su Wei keeps insisting. But he no longer can write fiction, he says. His imagination is barren, haunted only by images of Tiananmen. Instead, Su, along with tens of thousands of overseas Chinese, are left to wonder what went so wrong on June 4, 1989. I ask whether either of them regret their involvement in Tiananmen.

...

"Regret?" Li Jinjin smirks, as if I have asked something ridiculous. "No I'm not regretful."

...

"Regret?" Wang Juntao rolls the word around in his mouth, as one might do to fine wine, before spitting the word back out decisively. "Regret, guilt, these kinds of words, then it will eat you alive, nag at you. My attitude is if you don't do it good the first time, then you do it right the next time. Regret and other, similar things, I think it's a very unhealthy attitude."

...

"Regret?" Su Wei repeats back to me. "No regret! No, I don't regret anything I did! But that was not who I am then, I was not a politician."

Emily
Feng

...

"Regret?" Kang Zhengguo considers the question. "I realized I am a reactionary," he concludes. Not reactionary on the political spectrum, he explains. But "something in me is always pushing against the rules. It's in my nature and character to question. From the very beginning I've never been a political person. I've been a writer and through writing, I find truth."

Act V Reflection

That truth is elusive, however. The Tiananmen community is divided on how to remember Tiananmen. Were the students naive in thinking they could actually change the anachronistic Communist Party or did the protests really have a chance of success? Was it a movement of idealistic, self-sacrificing students or was it the movement of simultaneously narcissistic and naive students who thought they were immune to persecution? "The thing is," Liu Binyan, a famous Chinese journalist, once recounted, "they (the students) knew nothing about history. They thought they were the first democrats in China. But their greatest failing was their personal desire for power."

Within any large movement there will naturally be disagreement, but here has been an unusual level of vitriol among Tiananmen's former participants. The accusation of self-interest is exacerbated by the fact that the majority of Tiananmen's participants quickly melted back into Chinese society, understandably so, after the wave of questioning and arrests that followed June 4, and due to their high levels of education and intelligence, quite a few have risen to prestigious positions in business, academia and ironically, government.

Like the insidious viciousness of family infighting, the debate still continues in hushed, conspiratorial tones in private conversations, but the people I spoke with were either ambivalent or unconcerned about, though perhaps not unaware of, these doubts. Li Jinjin is quick to point out that he was "naive, in the sense that [he] never was interested in power" and Su Wei is eager to deny the accusations that he's made covert bargains he's made with China's leadership.

Thoughts on China's political future are just as diverse as those on its political past, refracted through the lenses of each individual participant. Despite their own participation in the Tiananmen protests, some see the agency of reform largely coming from the slow forming effects of modernization. "It's a Pandora's box of

in New York. "The girl was furious and yelled at me that I was irresponsible, like all Chinese intellectuals, who talk big and then duck the consequences of their words. I still can't figure it out. What she meant is that we fled! We fled!"

I do not observe the same guilt in the four participants I talked to, mostly, I believe, because each of them have found some way of maintaining a proactive relationship with their political pasts. Writing is the medium of redemption for Su Wei and Kang Zhengguo, who continue to remember and reconstruct the past; for Wang Juntao and Li Jinjin, the never-ending business of political reform was, is and will always be their connection to their homeland.

And there's plenty more of stories of how former Tiananmen exiles have parlayed their other talents into future success. There's the case of Chai Ling, one of the most visible of the former student vanguard. She moved to Paris and then the U.S., where she earned an MBA from Harvard and an honorary degree from Princeton, eventually founding a successful software learning company. Today she is the head and founder of a non-profit called All Girls Allowed that works to expose the human rights violations of China's one-child policy and most recently released an autobiographical work about her rags-to-riches story. Then there's Li Lu, another student leader during Tiananmen; today, he is a wildly successful hedge fund manager who at one point was in line to succeed Warren Buffet to manage a $100 billion portfolio. Finally, there is Shen Tong who ran an underground newspaper and radio broadcast operated straight out of his dorm room back in 1989. He managed to escape China a few days after the June 4 shooting, earning degrees at Brandeis and Boston University, and although he ran around in dissident circles for the first few years, his attention shifted decisively to commerce by the late 1990s. Today, he does lucrative business freely in China, where he sells Internet software that could either open up China's tightly-controlled web or tighten the screws even further, depending on who is using it.

Su describes his last visit to China, where he met with a number of close friends who had all become highly successful in government and business in the 24 years since Tiananmen. They were all very happy in their new lives, he described, though in private conversation they were eager to reminisce about their adventures as young, idealistic, swashbuckling protesters. "They were good friends, so they had no reason to lie. I think it is because people in China have double-faces; they put one face out to the public and wear another face in private."

This cognitively dissonant, doublethink ability is responsible for the bought silence of his peers. In some ways, Li Jinjin and Wang Juntao share similar views; both insinuate that Chinese people would otherwise be openly on their side, if not for the system of disincentives rallied against them.

Kang has encountered the same difficulties. "As soon as I thought of the people who had participated in Tiananmen, I had a very nostalgic feeling in my heart. But they did not want to talk about Tiananmen at all. A lot of people are like that; they had been struggled against, had suffered punishment. These people have all refused to talk about the circumstances to other people or raise the issue." In his memoirs, Kang writes about his first trip back to China after his exile, in 2000, where he met up with a few old friends from his teaching and labor camp days, who despite his best efforts to start conversation about Tiananmen preferred instead to discuss where to send their children to study abroad. "I simply could not engage my friends in a conversation about the Tiananmen protests," he writes. "Did they find the subject unduly depressing? What did I hope to gain by discussing it with them? How many people in China, with it bizarre juxtapositions of glory and corruption, had managed to remain idealistic in these hard-nosed times? Everyone insisted that China had changed beyond my understanding during my prolonged absence and that I should suspend all judgment for the time being."

He takes the analysis one step farther with me: "Americans have the American dream; now the Chinese have something called the Chinese dream. They have become more practical, more realistic; this is not a policy issue but just a development issue. I don't agree with Su Wei in saying that there are two sides. They may not have renounced their views but they have drawn a boundary. They cherish what's on the other side in their memories but have packed them away, like you put things in the refrigerator, to freeze them away. They are beginning their new life."

For many, as the spike in graduate school enrollment by Chinese students has shown, that new life meant coming to a new land as well: the United States. "It's hard to kill idealism. But Uncle Sam helped by rewarding extreme pragmatism. The green card is the best way to kill idealism," Wu'er Kaixi bluntly observed once in an interview.

But Li Jinjin looks genuinely perplexed when I ask him why so many other Tiananmen participants have released their political ties.

"I don't know...From my circle, no the people did not forget. I don't know why we're different maybe because Kang from different city, my circle might be more political than he is."

Hui Cui, the Peking student during the protests, puts the blame on a cultural flaw (or strength) particular to Chinese culture. "In China's almost 5,000 years of history, she has never initiated aggression but always defended herself from outside attack. We have developed an instinct to survive; survival is all that matters, and when things get better, we forget."

Act VII A Culture of Forgetting

For every one person who says something, one can easily find another that will disagree. "I don't think the Chinese have 'culture of forgetting.'" Li Jinjin dismisses my question, once again. "The Chinese people place one of the biggest importances on history. We are studiers of history. It's the Chinese media and government that try to make us forget. I don't feel forgotten because China is so big. Even 1% of people who are interested in this political event about history the number is still big."

Fang Lizhi, a democracy activist who died in April of last year, would disagree. While still in hiding at the American embassy in China, shortly after June 4, 1989, he wrote an essay called *"Communist Techniques of Amnesia."* The essay was published shortly after in the *New York Times Book Review*, though it was received with a certain measure of confusion. Wrote Perry Link, a friend of Fang's, and who has since done significant work on Tiananmen: "Why did Fang find this issue so salient at a time when world opinion was ablaze in revulsion at the massacre? Tiananmen was receiving plenty of attention – indeed much more attention than Fang and Li, in their sequestered state, could handle. Why was "forgetfulness" a problem?"

Fang describes his stymied efforts to hold a conference on the 1957 Anti-Rightest purge, his astonishment upon hearing that only fifteen years earlier, in 1942, the Communist party used the same methods of persecution against intellectuals at their base in Yan'an. "But fifteen years later my generation was completely ignorant of it. We deserved the ridicule we received," he writes. "After another thirteen years, in 1970, it became our turn to laugh," he remembers. The Cultural Revolution was coming to a close and the Red Guards, Mao's loyal student cadres, were now themselves the victims of political persecution, sent to the desolate countryside for "reeducation." Su Wei was one of these students. "Most of these

students, as innocent as I had been in 1957, never imagined that the Communist government could be so cruel in its treatment of students who had followed them so loyally," Fang observes. And in 1989, history repeated itself again.

The cyclical turbulence of China's last century of history is the result of a huge social experiment, brainwashing (the Chinese word, *xi nao*, literally means "to wash the head") on a massive scale. Contesting the truth becomes a he-said-she-said game; what do individual voices matter against the official account? These voices are numbered as well. "Today, the only things that are left are the memories the living, and only a fraction of the living want to remember," muses Kang.

But self-censorship cannot occur if the memory of repression is quickly forgotten; the Chinese public had to remember Tiananmen but only the official version, the memory kept salient while being prohibited from any public commemoration or discussion of the protests. The CCP began a huge, society-wide PR campaign to subvert and co-opt potentially dangerous interpretation of the events. The 1989 protests were quickly called a "counterrevolutionary rebellion" then to the more innocuous-sounding "events," which gradually became downgraded to "incident and finally "skirmish." The movement's most prominent voices were driven into hiding, where, in isolation, they could not contradict the Chinese government's assertions. Wang Juntao and Li Jinjin went into hiding before being caught; Su Wei quietly left the country after being tipped off; Kang Zhengguo was, once again, socially ostracized for his actions.

A silent understanding developed between the older Chinese generation and the political ruling class: only economic liberalization, not political liberalization, was on the table. Personal memories of Tiananmen 1989 were superseded by a standardized, public version in which the Communist government efficiently quashed a small group of selfish "hooligans" to the benefit of all. "When a government kills its own citizens, what can you do?" asks Hui Cui, the then- Peking university student. The answer to her question— *nothing at all* – was left unspoken, but hung uncomfortably in the air between us.

While the Chinese government strove to shape the collective memory of Tiananmen among those that had directly experienced the event, it simultaneously attempted to prevent any kind of historical memory to be passed on to generations born after 1989.

Curious, I asked around among the Chinese international graduate students, all of whom had been born before Tiananmen 1989. One, my language partner, looked at me with big, almost-childlike eyes, immediately serious. "I didn't know much at all before I came to the U.S. It's mentioned only very briefly in our textbooks, but it's one of those, what do you call it, sensitive topics that no one talks about." That's because the protests are barely mentioned or taught in the standardized curriculum for Chinese students. And "in this manner, about once each decade, the true face of history is thoroughly erased from the memory of Chinese society," Fang wrote prophetically in 1989.

Their success may be due less to their explicit attempts to edit history but from the unintended and (depending on whose side you are on) fortuitous consequences of China's "economic miracle." In 1992, Deng Xiaoping made his "Southern Tour" to Guangzhou, Shenzhen, Zhuhai and Shanghai, promoting his message of economic opening and reform. The campaign can be seen as a watershed date for the beginning of China's extended economic growth spurt. Regardless of whether Deng really proclaimed "to get rich is glorious," the prescient slogan quite accurately summarized what would follow.

"It is a fact that China has a big cultural problem, corruption problem. The government people always encourage people to make money. They control the media...the Chinese not healthy at this moment. It's safe for them to make money," Li Jinjin explains. China's fast-growing economy and the shocking materialism and hard-nosed pragmatism that has followed is probably a familiar story for most of us. It's certainly why so many Tiananmen participants have also given up politics.

Understanding human behavior in this paradigm of sticks and carrots, Wang Juntao and Li Jinjin harbor little resentment towards the lack of agency among their Chinese peers, though Wang admits he is sometimes a "little frustrated" with the apathy he encounters. "I don't expect that everyone will be political. I do feel a little bit frustrated about current Chinese corruptive culture," Li hedges.

Li even sounds slightly defensive when I mention the low levels of political dissent among mainland Chinese citizens. "It's very hard for individuals [to speak up] due to arrest, harassment, employment and of course currently it is very difficult for anyone to stand up requesting change to democracy because Communist party of China now has created the idea of *wei wen*. In English,

it means sustaining the stability of society is paramount. The government uses this as an excuse to wipe out anyone." And of course, much of the population has been bought off with the lucrative promise of financial opportunity in return for their tacit acceptance of the *status quo*.

Finding that others outside of their small community of dissidents and exiles still have interest in Chinese political history is thus extremely gratifying. In the middle of my interview with Kang, he checks his email. "I just received an email from a Chinese student at Berkeley," he explains. "She read my book and now she wants to talk about what happened. And today you come talk to me, so it is a good day." Kang smiles happily, content.

The (Iron) Curtain Falls

In some ways, outside of the pervasive influence of the exile has been a liberation of sorts. "I was able to write it because I was in America. I had more perspective, I could see over my own walls. The distance set me free," Su Wei once remarked about his novel, *Witching Vale*. Su remembers how he used to joke, "How many people get the chance to be exiles? How romantic!" We're proud of ourselves, to tell the truth. Here we are, facing down one of the most powerful governments in the world, and we can stand here and say, I don't care! And meanwhile they're watching our every move. And so in a way that's proof of our own power."

I realize that I am talking to a special subset of people; not only were they lucky to leave China in the first place, but they have "survived—" mentally, emotionally, physically. That Li Jinjin and Wang Juntao were able to endure harsh, sometimes multiple, prison sentences speaks to an innate toughness that made starting over a bearable challenge. And in some senses, the exiles have not really left China. "In the US I'm in a difference space. In my office, I speak Chinese, I speak in Chinese with my students who are good enough to not use English. It is as if I used a magnet to transport my Chinese here. Very rarely do I hear English. Geographically I am away, but culturally I have not left," Kang explains. "Politically, culturally mentally I still believe that I'm China," Li Jinjin corroborates. "I'm writing I'm thinking; everything is about China."

That China is less political than it is cultural. Su explains, "there are three Chinas. The first is its long history and cultural traditions; both I love. The second is its people, who I also love. And the third is its government, which I hate!" Indeed, the impression I received

was that the Communist government was an unwanted intrusion, a blemish on the true character of China's polity. In 2000, as if to illustrate this point, Kang became a naturalized U.S. citizen; his Chinese citizenship was just too much of a "liability" and was meaningless anyway, since he remains Chinese in heart and mind. Even if these four exiles and their historical peers may tell incongruent narratives about Tiananmen, they all agree that China's story, whether from an individual or society level standpoint, must continue being told, because the happy ending they all hope for is not in sight yet.

But for most viewers, the show ended as soon as the first gunshots were fired the night of June 4, 1989. The sudden extinguishing of the protests had the nightmarish quality of a bad horror film as soldiers fired on bystanders and Beijing citizens pitched improvised street battles with troops. When the world woke up the next day, the nightmare was quickly dismissed as just that—a mere dream whose unreal quality was reinforced by state-run censorship. Only a fraction of the audience remains watching the show now, despite the fact that the story has not yet ended. And even for those who obstinately remember, keeping the truth alive is a task unto itself. As the wife of Fang Lizhi, Li Shuxian offhandedly observed about the state of exile: "You know, I used to be a good teacher, but here there is no one for me to teach. Now, I am finally free to talk, but there is no one for me to talk to."

Emily
Feng

The Hallyu[8] Wave Finally Arrives in America

An exploration into themes and currents behind the sudden explosion of the K-Pop hit song Gangnam Style on the American scene prompts writers and commentators to ask the question: Why now? Why PSY? Why Gangnam-style?

With Gangnam assumed into the chief media export, of South Korea, the rotund, bespectacled and equine-admiring PSY's Gangnam-Style is replete with the implications of rampant wealth and affluence tied to the term and the lyrics of the song. Yet a more careful look at its themes reveals the song's journey and the contrasts in cultural constants of both Korea and the west.

Disclaimer: The English lyrics on the right are my own translations, and the opinions and interpretations of cultural trends presented in this paper are also my own analysis so please don't take this essay as an official stance.

Christine Lee is a junior double majoring in Neuroscience and History of Science and Technology at Duke. She loves puppies, writing, and ice cream crepes.

117

"Eh - Sexy Lady."
Gangnam Style is a Korean Pop (K-Pop) song composed and sung by PSY, a prominent artist employed by JYP Entertainment, arguably the most elite management company in Asia. At first, I must admit, I was not impressed. To be honest, watching a music video featuring a particularly ugly middle-aged Asian man in a bright suit, dancing like a horse and singing inane lyrics about romance is not really my idea of inspiring music. Alas, this was what I was greeted with after coming back from a techonlogy-less summer trip. One day, I was boiling my water to kill parasites because there was no filtering system, and the next, I was listening to auto-tuned electronic music with flashing disco lights.

"지금부터 갈 데까지 가볼까."　　　　**Let's go to the top.**

Believe it or not, my conservative post-middle-age parents introduced me to this trendy new techno song. Korean artists have been trying to "break" the American market for as long as I can remember. In fact my first concert was part of a K-Pop world tour featuring the then-hottest Korean singers and dancers; I was still in elementary school when my parents took me there to familiarize me with the contemporary culture of their homeland. However, no Korean artists ever succeeded becoming even moderately popular amongst the wider American audience that doesn't include the eccentric K-pop fanatics, until now. For the reason of national pride alone, on my first day back from abroad, my parents thought it an absolute necessity to force upon me PSY's single, the first Korean song to rise to the top of the iTunes charts.

"오빠 강　　남스타"　　　　**Oppa[1] is Gangnam style.**

The chorus repeats over again and over again down the dorm halls of fraternity houses, but in order to fully understand the meaning and implications behind Gangnam, one needs some background on recent Korean history. In 1950, Korea began a civil war that grew into epic proportions involving world superpowers like China, the Soviet Union, and the United States. The conflict eventually split the already tiny nation into two smaller fragments. Even today North and South Korea are technically still in a state of war, but with the precarious label

[1] Oppa is how females address older brothers or males in their family. However, it may also be used to address an older male, with whom the female has a particularly close relationship.

"stalemate"[2] masking the underlying hostilities that still resound in the hearts of its peoples. Especially because they have developed into such different countries culturally, economically, and governmentally, the contrast between the two can be seen clearest when comparing Pyongyang and Seoul, the capitals of North and South Korea respectively. While Pyongyang exudes a foreboding militaristic aura with the strongly evident censorship policy and perceivable scarcity in the dress, manner and shops of its people, Gangnam (which literally means "south of the river") is a Seoul district located on the southern side banks of the Hangang, renowned for its display of obscene wealth.

"뛰는놈그위에나는놈."	**Above the running man is the flying man.**

As South Korea developed under a series of dictators and democratic reforms, the building of infrastructure allowed for innovative entrepreneurs to lay the groundwork for companies that would become leaders in technology within a span of 50 years. These financial moguls began leading industry powerhouses such as Samsung, LG, Hyundai, and Kia, which bolstered the economy of South Korea and precipitated its rapid rise from a third-world developing country to one included in the selective G20, a group of countries possessing the most influential global economies. Originally, Gangnam was an underdeveloped area of Seoul, but because companies needed land to build headquarters and factories, Gangnam was established as the main home financial district. Now, Gangnam is considered the wealthiest part of Seoul, on par with Upper East Side in New York.

"나는 사나이."[3]	**I am a manly man.**

So what is Gangnam style? Gangnam style refers to the wealthy, materialistic lifestyle currently sought after by the young Korean generation. In the lyrics of the song, PSY only refers to one female character, the original sexy lady whom he desperately searches for by advertising his status as a single Gangnam-style man. However, from the beginning of the music video, it seems as though he has access to plenty of women, often seen through scenes in which he is the only male surrounded by a harem of attractive female characters. For example, in the indoor horse ring, he is prominently shown as the sole man dancing in a group of scantily clad women. In addition, he waddles his way along the Hangang river, leering at the yoga-practicing women. Even in the party

---

[2] Stalemate may not be the currently politically correct term. I am taking rough translations of what my parents have told me in Korean.
[3] 사나이 directly translates to boy, but in this context means a raw man's man.

Christine
Lee

bus, a scene that lacks the overt sexuality that is present throughout the video, PSY can be see thrusting his hips surrounded by older ajummas.[4] These suggestive clips imply that the epitome of a Gangnam-style man is a materialistic philanderer. This reflects the nature of male dominance and patriarchal hierarchy of Korean society, in which there exists a deeply historically rooted double standard for promiscuity in men and women.

"그래 너 **hey** 그래 바로 너."   **Yes you, hey that's right, you.**

When attempting to understand this song, I realized that you have to do it along with the video itself because the irony of the lyrics can only truly be seen when juxtaposed against the clips that go along with them. After realizing that, I found two visual themes that seemed to be particularly odd to me: horses and sunglasses, which were featured so prominently within the music video, but not mentioned at all in the lyrics. In South Korea, horses are a nowadays a key trademark of the rich. Due to the dearth of land, the ability to buy into a country club with enough land to support a stable, let alone trails and fields to practice recreational horseback riding, implies exceptional affluence. Therefore, the horse-themed video may be an exhibition of the wealth that Gangnam citizens are purported to have. The sunglasses may just be a reflection of the pretentiousness that is inherent in the Gangnam style. Throughout the entire video, even in the scene where he meets his lady love, PSY never shows his eyes, the supposed windows to the soul. Thus, this deliberate choice in costuming may be a statement about how Gangnam style refers to a superficial outer shell, without any substance or soul.

"그런 반전 있는 여자."   **A girl with different faces.**

So essentially this song is about a man who describes himself a worthy man looking for a "sexy" lady presumably, the woman of his dreams. She is described as "a girl who is appropriately meek but becomes fun and wild when the situation arises,"[5] and he describes himself as one who "seems calm on the surface but becomes crazy when the right time comes."[6] In both characters referred to by the lyrics, there seems to inherently be two dimensions: a calm side and a wild side. Due to the strong Confucian influence of the culture's heritage, even today in Korea, women are considered to be more desirable when meek, quiet, and quaint. Similarly

---

[4] Ajumma refer to a middle-aged woman as depicted in the video by the curly headed women with visors-- typically they are married with kids and are usually housewives.
[5] 정숙해 보이지만 놀 땐 노는 여자, 이때다 싶으면 묶었던 머리 푸는 여자.
[6] 점잖아 보이지만 놀 땐 노는 사나이, 때가 되면 완전 미쳐버리는 사나이.

men are more respected when they portray the image of calmness and scholarliness ("a man who has bulging imagination rather than bulging muscles"[7]). The lyrics seem to suggest the feelings of a young man torn between a conflict in his own personality. Because social norms dictated by older generations indicate the appeal of a calm, collected persona, but western influence has also created a culture emphasizing the necessity of sex appeal and a certain level of party-craziness that directly contrasts childhood indoctrination of moral values. Therefore, a closer look at Gangnam Style shows a satire that the younger generation in South Korea may understand about the suppression of inner feelings and personalities for the sake of propriety.

"커피 한잔의 여유를 아는 품격있는 여자 밤이 오면 심장이 뜨거워지는 여자"
A girl who knows how to drink coffee freely, but at night whose heart becomes hot.

Coffee shops are plentiful in Seoul, because they are so profitable. Koreans have become obsessed with the concept of a coffee break, originally a western idea. Lounging in a coffee shop while reading a book has become a standard classy activity. During the Korean War, to "protect" South Korea, the United States established a military base there, which precipitated an almost one-way cultural exchange in which western influence through radio, TV, and music flooded the Korean Peninsula. At the time, Americans were significantly wealthier, so rich Koreans tried to emulate them, and then like a trickle-down effect, the poor Koreans tried to emulate the rich Koreans which resulted in creating a cultural trend that to be westernized was to be desirable. Not only has coffee become popular, night clubs with laser lights, yoga as a recreational activity, and party buses are all also US imports now present in mainstream Korean culture. Even the girl who PSY becomes enraptured by in the end has dyed orange hair and unnaturally light skin. From the back or from very far away, one might even mistake her for an American with Irish roots.

"You know what I'm saying"

From my perspective, the Gangnam Style phenomenon is a powerful statement about the effects of globalization on both Korean and American

---

[7] 근육보다 사상이 울퉁불퉁한 사나이.
[8] Hallyu is a play on phonetics; it's supposed to mimic the Asian pronunciation of Hollywood. Essentially the Hallyu wave refers to anything regarding the modern mass entertainment media industry in Asia.

culture. Koreans and Korean immigrants such as my parents, who came to America to work as adults, view it as a triumph. After relatively recently suffering under difficult post-war conditions, they are proud that Koreans have accomplished so much in such a short period of time to become accepted by mainstream America, their role model country. On the other hand, I and those of my generation who have grown up in a mixed Korean and American household background, observe so many parallels between this video and the standard American pop songs such as those by Lady Gaga that also feature many of the same visual themes (i.e. bright colors and overwhelming extravagance). Rather, it is the elements of traditional Korean culture that are barely present, if at all in this viral music video. It's such a shame, especially because there is a rich history of more than five thousand years that could have been incorporated. Ultimately, the most pointed joke may be on the unaware Americans who seem to be the original progenitor of materialistic culture, so self-obsessed that they only like things that are a reflection of themselves.

Acknowledgements

I would like to thank my writing group (Shyla Saini, Julijana Englander, Allison Kratka, and Meghan Thomas) for all of their thoughtful comments and edits. I would also like to thank Professor Joseph Harris for helping me choose a direction for this piece. In addition, the following persons/ entities positively influenced the final version of this paper: Suellen Li, Writing Studio, Claire Li, Sean Ji, and my father.

Work Cited

PSY. "PSY - GANGNAM STYLE (M/V)." YouTube. YouTube, 15 July 2012. Web. 12 Oct. 2012. <http://www.youtube.com/watch?v=9bZkp7q19f0>.

Encircle 包围
PART I – Patients & Messages

As many scholars have noted, history inevitably centers on struggles for power. Accordingly historical textbooks, and thus the students of the world, see the past through the lens of politics, warfare, and economics. On the one hand these large scale perspectives are an attempt to capture and explain the movements in world history that impact the most people: regime changes, economic policies, and war have instantaneously changed the fates of hundreds of millions of individuals. However, this view of history also simplifies the past to a mere collection of political, economic, and militaristic decisions. Such a paradigm fundamentally denies the individual agency that constitutes an important part of history. When parsing through this history, questions arise in the mind almost automatically: Who lived here? What were their names? What did they eat? What did they think about the world around them? When did they get married, and what were familial relations like? The answers to these questions, in the aggregate, constitute the actual experiences of individuals living in a certain epoch.

This piece seeks to solidify the link between the center and the periphery of historical experience by telling a tale that, while fictional, draws heavily from primary source materials. In doing so, I hope this tale depicts the lived-experience of the people who made that history. In writing the story of the brothers Yuan Ming 元明 and Yi Han 毅涵, the questions it sought to answer were: What role did a random villager from rural China have during the Purge of 1937? From the lens of future generations, what role do any of us play in the creation of our past and present? Do we have a voice?

Ian Zhang *is a rising senior at Duke University currently pursuing a joint degree in History, Chinese, & Computer Science. Ian was born at Duke Hospital while his father was pursuing a PhD in Cell Biology at Duke Medical Center. The Zhang family relocated to Mercer Island WA, where Ian spent his school years. He soon discovered he had a deep passion for literature, history, and culture. At Duke he underwent an identity crisis as he re-navigated his relationship with his cultural heritage: a key theme in his writing which often deals with the complexity of East-West relations. Outside of school Ian plays water polo for Duke, serves as, President of IGC & actively seeks out entrepreneurial projects. Ian plans on working in China for a few years post-graduation before pursuing a law degree.*

*The author is available to answer any questions or comments at **ian.zhang@duke.edu***

I. Shanghai, Southeast China: April 9th 1927

Shadows made long by a sliver of crescent moon reached out from behind the slanting stone barrier. A hazy flood of grey moonlight was all that illuminated my path to the Old City wall[1], seemingly announcing my presence as an unwelcome intruder. Clutching the handle of my briefcase tightly I hurried towards the exit.

"Stop," declared a voice.

The statement was accompanied by the distinct *click* of a Mauser C96.[2] Straining my eyes, I caught movement in the shadows directly in front of me. My heart began pounding erratically. *They know.*

I froze midstride, caught in an exposing beam of moonlight while unable to peer into the thick shadows that surrounded me. "I-I'm a doctor," I stammered, glancing nervously around. The unsettling notion of a long, smooth gun barrel just a few feet away in the dark, aimed at my head, did nothing to quell the erratic pounding in my chest.

"Did you not hear the news?" the voice sneered, "no one's allowed out of the Old City after dark, not even doctors." Derisive snorts of laughter rang out from behind the voice. I guessed there were three others, maybe more.

"I've been called to see an extremely sick patient in the French Concession," I replied.

"Open your bag," the voice demanded immediately.

Unwilling tremors traveled the length of my arm as I slowly placed the black briefcase on the ground in front of my feet and unzipped it. Nearby shadows stirred slightly as the silvery barrel of a gun slid into view, followed immediately by a uniformed guard. A dark wool cap cast a deep shadow over the man's face, but the coffee colored hue of a cleanly pressed military jacket and

---

[1] *View of the Walled City. 1910. Photograph. Shanghai. Virtual Shanghai. Web. 12 Dec. 2012.* A photo of the walls of the Old City, or Chinese section, of Shanghai in the early 20th century.
[2] *Fortier, David M. "Giant .45 Broomhandle From China." Gun World Feb. 2001: 1-6. Web. 13 Dec. 2012.* A magazine article that discusses the extensive use of the Mauser C96 by Chinese armed forces in the early 20th century.

matching trousers told me he was a man of some ranking. Not all Nationalist soldiers were fortunate enough to own an official military ensemble. [3]

More shadows parted behind him, revealing several languid-looking characters wielding an assortment of axes, pistols, and rusty swords. One stepped forward and spat a dirty glob of saliva at my feet. Other than the soldier, the rest looked unkempt, restless, gangsters. *These Nationalist pigs are not even trying to hide the fact that they're working with the Green Gang thugs anymore.*[4] I could barely contain my disgust.

The soldier approached cautiously. The gun was steady in his grip, performing a slow 90-degree arc around me as he took in the two-piece wool suit,[5] the black character asserting "Doctor" painted on the papers protruding from the breast pocket, and finally craned his neck to examine the contents of the now open bag. As he leaned in the two stars on his collar glinted dimly in the hazy night: a Lieutenant Colonel. A moment passed before he pointed and motioned at my breast pocket with his gun.

Eyes fixated on the barrel, I carefully handed him the folded documents, the contents of which I had begun memorizing that morning when I had accepted the assignment. *Doctor Pan, Harbin County, Shaan Xi Province, 2nd Medical Schoo-* my recitation was interrupted by a brief motion of the gun, signaling me to continue through to the exit.

"All right, doctor, let's see where you're going," the soldier said. The emphasis he placed on my supposed title left no doubt in my mind that he was yet to be convinced by my disguise.

I picked up my briefcase and began trudging through the west gate. The nearly silent tread of military issue boots indicated the guard, and his gun, were not far behind. The clink of rusty weapons and the low, guttural tones of the gangsters followed us through into the French Concession, but the rest of the streets were deathly

[3] Teng, Xinyun. *Kang Zhan Shi Qi Lu Jun Fu Zhi Zhuang Bei 1931-1945.* Tai Bei Xian: Lao Zhan You Gong Zuo Shi Chu Ban, 90. 14-76. Print. Included a large number of photos of different military uniforms of the time covering Nationalist, Communist, and different warlord factions.
[4] Wilbur, C. Martin. "The Nationalist Revolution: from Canton to Nanking, 1923–28." 12-15, 104-112, 136-138. Republican China 1912–1949, Part 1. Ed. John K. Fairbank. Cambridge University Press, 1983. Cambridge Histories Online. 12 December 2012. A detailed account of the intricate link between General Chiang Kai-Shek and the gangsters of Shanghai. Recounts how his previous residence in the city allowed him to cultivate connections with some of the more notorious characters in the city. Also describes specific acts of sabotage and violence
[5] A Portrait of Chen Qimei. 1910. Photograph. Shanghai. Virtual Shanghai. Web. 12 Dec. 2012. Many western-inclined or higher stratum individuals would wear western-style suits in Shanghai.

Ian
Zhang

quiet. It seemed news of the newly imposed martial law had traveled quickly.[6] As we exited the Old City and crossed the street, I looked up to see a sign pointing south indicating "Margaret Williamson Hospital." I tacked left as the shadows suddenly retracted, replaced instead by a broad swath of moonlight.

Shanghai's French Concession sprawled out before me. This once small residential area had exploded in the wake of the First World War. The sprawling tracks of the Shanghai South Railway Station lay just below the Concession, feeding into a series of tram routes that ran throughout the Concession and into the international district beyond. Grey brick-and-mortar houses and shops lined the paved streets. The dotted white marble columns, three-squared brick residences, and Western-style villas reflected the migration of British and American merchants into the French Concession while high-rising church spires were a testament to the growing Russian presence. Schools, power stations, and country clubs were on every street corner. , ,

I stopped abruptly outside the doors of the Margaret Williamson Hospital. The six-building complex was just outside Shanghai's Old City and just inside the French Concession, placing it a crossroads of sorts between the Chinese and foreign presence. Built a mere five years earlier, the hospital and its staff reflected this intersection well, composed of a mixed crew of native Chinese nurses and western Evangelical missionaries.

I jumped as my uniformed accompaniment knocked on the gate with the barrel of his Mauser. His ill-groomed companions lounged a few steps away, leaning against a wall passing a cigarette between them. The door creaked open slowly, and a short-statured, timid-looking nurse glanced first at me, then at the armed guard standing next to me. Her eyes darted between his gun and face.

Perhaps recognizing that she was not a danger to him, the soldier holstered his gun and asked, "Nurse, this man says he was called here…"

As he deliberately trailed off I tensed up. If things had not been arranged correctly on the other side, the situation could deteriorate quickly. The nurse stared once again at the Nationalist's gun, then at my face, saying nothing. The silence wore on and a look of understanding began to creep over the soldier's face. I saw his hand

---

[6] *Wakeman, Frederic E. Policing Shanghai, 1927-1937. Berkeley: University of California, 1995. Print. Describes the imposition of martial law in Shanghai on April 9th, 1927 to drive out radicals under the guise of maintaining law and order.*

reaching slowly down to his waist. Keeping an eye on the ruffians lounging against the wall, my mind began churning as to how best to get the concealed gun at the bottom of my black briefcase out. I started to hedge towards the front door for potential cover.

Suddenly, just as his hand was about to reach the handle of the gun, the nurse stepped quickly through the door, placing herself in between the two of us. "Yes, we have been expecting Doctor Pan," she said with a tremor in her voice. She continued, "there is a seriously ill patient here and Doctor Pan has received some training in treating her disease."

The soldier gave the nurse a long look. "I see," he replied after a long pause. After another sweeping glance at the pair of us, he barked out an order and began walking back towards the Old City with the others in tow. After watching them disappear out of sight, I turned to the nurse. "Thank yo—" I began, but she cut me off, all sense of fear gone.

"Come inside Comrade," she said, as she ushered me inside the door. Surprised at the sudden shift in her demeanor, I stepped into a darkened hallway, trying to let my eyes adjust. I quickly felt the firm hand of the nurse on my arm. "This way," she said, "your brother is waiting."

I let her lead me through the silent hallways and up a staircase. The rooms we passed were dimly lit, most of the beds empty. My mind filled with questions as to who this comrade was. Though after the May Thirtieth movement the party had swelled to more than 20,000 due to the inclusion of women and the laboring class, the Communist presence in Shanghai was still based mostly on interpersonal relations and former connections established before the First World War. I wanted to ask her where she was from, but the silence of the hospital dissuaded me. I racked my brains trying to think of whether I was connected to her in some way, but eventually just settled on the fact that she was another addition to the movement, and that meant we were one step closer to revolutionizing the country.

We had stopped at the beginning of a short corridor. The nurse turned to me and said, "the last room on the right."

"Thank you comrade," I responded. I hesitated, wanting to ask her where she was from, but she had already begun walking back down the staircase.

Turning towards the direction she had indicated, I walked the few steps down the hallway and slowly pushed open the door on

Ian
Zhang

my right. I barely had time to register a brightly lit and sparsely furnished office before my hand was grasped firmly. The handshake turned into a full embrace as I heard my brother speak: "Yi Han, it's been too long."

"Yuan Ming, it really has," I replied, trying with difficulty to keep the emotion out of my voice. It had been almost two years since I had last seen my brother. I put my hands on his shoulders, taking in the sharply drawn features and aristocratic nose that had earned him the constant torment of our peers in school. "Foreign Devil," they would call him. When he came home crying from the incidents our parents would always smile and say, "foreigners can be good people too." When they passed a few years later, he ventured often into the international districts of the city, but he would never tell me what for. I looked into his eyes to see him scrutinizing me with equal intensity, perhaps reminiscing about the same times. His face mirrored the thought crossing my mind: so much had changed, yet so much had stayed the same.

"Did anyone give you trouble on the way here?" he asked. "With the martial law in place I wasn't sure you'd be able to get through to the French Concession."

"To be honest we've been expecting some sort of action from General Chiang. The Zhili clique has been running scared ever since the worker uprisings last month, so no sight of them. And the Party isn't nearly militarized enough. The Nationalists are the only ones with any sort of real power now."

"So no one gave you trouble at the gate?" he asked.

"A Nationalist soldier and some Green Gang thugs gave me some trouble coming out of the Old City, but the nurse at the front salvaged the situation. The forged doctoral papers were a genius idea Yuan Ming," I said.

"You should thank Colonel Ruo," he said as he smiled wanly. "He took care of all the paperwork." Looking at him more closely, I noticed my older brother did not have the excited look of a man fresh from victorious battle. I took a quick glance around the office as I sat down in a chair facing the lone window across from the door, noting the messy pile of loose papers on the desk and a framed photograph on the wall of what looked to be a missionary. Just outside the window I could see the stark metal lines of the power station rising a few blocks away.

"How was the Northern Expedition?" I queried, "tell me all about

the defeat of the warlords! We've been starved for information here. Is it true you sent those foreign devils back to their ships in Nanjing?"

Upon hearing my questions he turned slowly away from me, slumping into the chair at the desk. I saw the new stripes on his shoulder as he turned. With his back turned to me, I thought I glimpsed just the tiniest sliver of gray hair protruding from the back of his head. Gray hairs at 28.

Turning to face me, meeting my eyes slowly, he began, "Do you remember what I said to you after Mom and Dad died in the earthquake?"

"Of course," I said, a bit taken back. "We stick together, no matter what."

He nodded slowly. "That's right," he agreed. As if measuring his next words extremely carefully, he said, "The expedition was not what I expected." The syllables came slowly, deliberately. "We have a problem," he finished expectantly, looking up at me.

Sensing something was not quite right, I dropped my bag and leaned forward in my chair. "What happened?" I asked quietly.

Leaning forward, touching his fingertips together, he responded, "The initial plan fell through. It was supposed to be a joint operation between the two parties, Nationalist and Communist, working together to overthrow the warlord factions. The Communists were to lay the groundwork in each city, organizing labor protests, speaking to merchant unions, bringing in peasants from the countryside, and gathering intelligence. We Nationalists would come in after with military force."

"But isn't that exactly what happened?" I cut in. "We heard the reports trickle in from Wuhan and Nanchang. The Communists roused the people, inspiring them with our revolutionary fervor to drive out the imperialists and warlords, and your Nationalists came in and finished the job! Soon, the Nationalists, the whole country, will see how irresistible the class struggle is, they'll come around. It's happening in Shanghai right now—"

Yuan Ming held up his hand: "Please, let me finish," he said. Again, with the air of measuring his words carefully, he continued, "General Chiang has had a change of heart."

Not quite sure if I understood him correctly, I gave him a quizzical look. "A change of heart?" I asked, "about what? We've been preparing for his arrival in Shanghai for the past month. Labor unions have

been organized, the Zhili faction has pretty much been run out of town, the merchants are all on our side. What do you mean 'change of heart?'" my voice escalated, "he's due to arrive in the city in two days!"

Yuan Ming sat back in his chair, heaving out a long, drawn-out sigh, running his hands through his hair. "These last two years, the Nationalist leadership has been divided…"

"Yes, yes," I said impatiently, "Wang Jingwei is more sympathetic to the Communist cause and General Chiang wants to separate the two parties. But what does this have to do with a change of heart? We are still one bloc as set down by the Soviet Comintern, ready to overthrow the corrupt imperialists and warlords and reunite China under the banner of the mass—" ,

I started in my seat as the resounding smack of both of my elder brother's hands forcefully came into contact with the desk in front of him. "This is not the time for ideology and textbooks Yi Han! This is war!" As he glanced at my face with a smoldering glare his look softened. "This is family," he said. Now looking more calmly into my eyes, he said, "General Chiang has confided in a few of his highest-ranking officers, most of them like me—graduates from the Whampoa Military Academy." Relaxing back into his chair, Yuan Ming continued softly, "What I am about to tell you, you will not repeat to anyone. Do you understand?"

Still stinging from his rebuke, I nodded curtly. "Yes," I replied, "I understand."

Noticing my tone, Yuan Ming smiled wryly at me. "Little brother, not much has changed has it?"

Remembering all the times he had scolded me in the past, I couldn't help but allow a slight smile to crease my face as well. "No," I chuckled, "not mu—"

We both froze as a cacophony of harsh tones split the quiet night. Yuan Ming's neck snapped towards the window as he stood up, scattering the loose leaf papers on the desk. Unintelligible words and syllables escalated rapidly in volume as he stuck his head outside and glanced up and down the street. A split second later, he whipped back around and dove on the ground, yelling, "Get down!"

I tipped over my chair to the side as the sound of a gunshot rent the still night air. A moment passed before the situation dawned on both of us.

"Grab your bag!" a now wide-eyed Yuan Ming hissed at me while he scrambled to collect the loose sheaves of paper scattered all over the table. I ran to my bag and grabbed the handle as the distinct sound of doors being slammed open came from the floor beneath us. I stayed on the ground, frozen in my hesitation before I felt Yuan Ming's hand pulling on my shoulder.

I turned to see him already halfway through the door, the speed of his exit causing some of the loose papers in his grip to float out of his hands. Glancing back over my shoulder I stayed on my hands and knees and scurried out the door to follow him. Below us, the guttural shouts and the shattering sound of rifle butts being thrust through windowpanes echoed loudly. The sounds of broken glass chased us into the corridor and down the staircase. As I hit the bottom floor I glanced around: it was pandemonium. Patients and a few nurses in their nightgowns were standing or cowering in the hallway at random locations. Broken glass was littered everywhere. I barely made out a crumpled figure on the floor, blood pooling from her waist. A shadowy figure at the entrance to the hospital shouted. I looked straight at him as he raised a rifle to his shoulder. A bullet whizzed by my briefcase and something glass behind me shattered into pieces as I ducked down.

From the corner of my eye I saw Yuan Ming scramble straight across the hallway into a dark room. I hurried to follow. Once in the room I pulled up to an abrupt halt. He had stopped suddenly in front of me; I panicked for a brief moment as we reached the far wall of the room. It was a dead end. I desperately looked around for another exit as the excited sound of discovery emanated from the hallway we had just escaped. At the same moment Yuan Ming raised his right leg and shoved hard into the wall: a whole corner of the sidewall crumbled instantly under the force of his boot. He ducked through to the other side swiftly and as I followed suit I glimpsed down and saw the remnants of a cleverly concealed drywall.

A sliver of crescent moon greeted me on the other side: we were outside of the hospital facing the west end of the French Concession. Yuan Ming's hand pulled me behind him as he guided me to the right. The sounds of chaos gradually faded as we pounded down three separate side streets. I started to notice some familiar buildings, and was expecting to run into the French Concession street market before I heard a ragged "stop," uttered behind me. The night had become still once more.

Panting, the black bag swinging alongside, I whispered "Which way?"

Shaking his head vigorously and catching his breath, Yuan Ming bent over for a few moments. I thought he had started to rest before he straightened back up, with his left boot now in his hand. He tossed the boot at me while shifting the remaining sheaves of paper in his hands into a pile on the ground. As he lit the papers on fire he turned and said quickly, "Leave the French Concession from behind the market and head back to the Old City. There is a message for Colonel Ruo in the boot. You must get it to him tonight."

"But, where are you going?" I asked panting. "Who were those soldiers? Were they Nationalists?" What the hell is happening, I wondered.

"Just open the boot. It will explain everything," he gasped out. "I'll come to the Old City tomorrow to get you. Stay safe. Tell no one."

As another gunshot suddenly split the night air, I hurriedly shed my left boot and worked Yuan Ming's up and over my foot.

"Go!" he hissed at me as I looked around.

Sticking close to the long shadows afforded by the buildings lining the street, I began moving towards the market square. My heart pounding, I glanced behind me. I saw my brother's dark, uniformed silhouette, missing a shoe, outlined by the dim moon. The pile of ashes at his feet was blowing away in the wind. Not until I left the French Concession did I remember there was a gun at the bottom of my bag.

.

.

.

.

to be continued

Correspondence:
Workers of the World's Factory

Fei Gao *is a Duke Senior double majoring in International Comparative Studies and Asian and Middle Eastern Studies; while also minoring in Cultural Anthropology. She is especially interested in the contemporary culture and politics of China, especially in how human rights issues affect both laborers within China and consumers of Chinese products in the rest of the world. She hopes to work in a factory for a month to gain some personal experience and a more in-depth view of this topic. Her ultimate goal is to produce research results that will not only add to the academic discourse, but help push for practical change.*

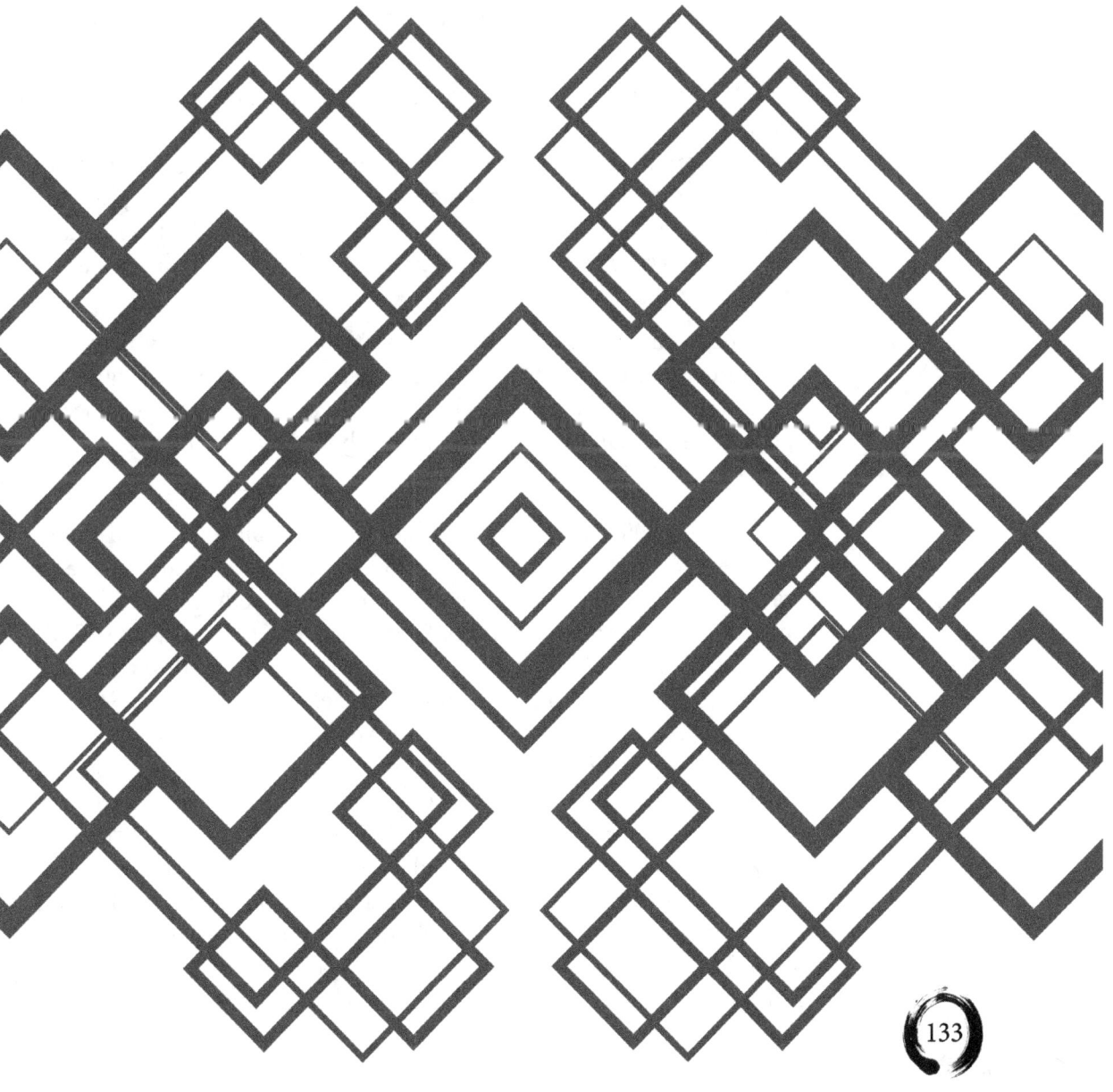

For the past two decades, Deng Xiaoping's economic reform policies have led to the biggest rural to urban migration in human history, turning China into the "world factory." However, as China awed the world with its rapid economic development, reports generally fail to mention the millions of internal-migrant workers who will not be able to take advantage of this economic boom. Those who made a significant contribution to China's growing economy are in fact the same people who are living on the fringes of society and working in horrific conditions in factories, in construction sites, and so on.

Only in recent years have scholars begun to study and understand this population that's often hidden from view - voiceless and without representation. In 2010, Foxconn, the world's largest contract electronic manufacturer for major brand names such as Apple, Dell and Toshiba, caught the world's attention when thirteen young migrant workers in Shenzhen attempted suicide all within a period of five months.

In the summer of 2013, I set out on a two-month journey, traveling through six different cities in China, in an attempt to understand the labor activism issues there. Below is an account of my experience at the Southern Sparrow NGO in Guangzhou, Guangdong, China.

Ding! The elevator came to a halt, and the silver-colored doors slid open. We had reached the fourth floor, and I stepped out to see a washed-up, light blue banner hanging from the ceiling. Ten Chinese characters, written in red and outlined in white, read 南飛社會工作服務部 *Nan Fei Yan She Hui Gong Zuo Fu Wu Bu*, with its English translation underneath, in a smaller, black font: *Southern Sparrow Social Work Service Center*. This non-government organization (NGO) based in Guangzhou, Guangdong was established in December of 2009 with the purpose of safeguarding the rights and interests of migrant laborers by providing free legal advice and litigation courses to workers and their families. Its main goal was to enhance the workers' legal awareness, thus empowering them to demand better treatment. I first heard about them two weeks ago. After several attempts at arranging a visit, the opportunity for one finally arose when the main director, Xu Xiaobo, told me about today's law

consulting session for local migrant workers. I had been picturing this moment all morning - what the office space would look like, how the migrant workers would act, how the law advisers would explain China's complicated legal system in colloquial language, but nothing prepared me for what I was about to experience.

There was no air conditioning inside, and I could feel my cotton tee-shirt clinging to my back as soon as I stepped into the hall. Without much hesitation, I strode up to three NGO workers sitting behind a long table with sign-in sheets. One of them lifted her head up, bit off a dry flake of skin from her bottom lip, and smiled. She looked like she was around my age, with rounded shoulders, and was wearing a light blue Southern Sparrow t-shirt that was way too big for her. She had thick bangs that reached past her eyebrows, completely covering her forehead, and the rest of her long, black hair was pulled back in a loose pony tail. As I walked closer, I could clearly see a trail of sweat trickling down the side of her face, causing her thick-rimmed glasses to slide down repeatedly. "Hello! I'm Gao Fei, a third year college student from the U.S." I introduced myself, "I spoke on the phone with Miss Xu yesterday, and she suggested that I come observe today's law consulting session." Her eyes lit up in recognition. In one swift, continuous motion, she gave a slight nod, pushed up her glasses, and stuck out both hands to shake mine: "Hello, hello! Welcome! Did you find this place okay? Come in, come in, sit down and join us."

Xu guided me into one of the conference rooms, which was already filled with fifty or so migrant workers. A sour smell of sweat reached my nostrils, and I fought back the urge to cringe. Large windows stretched across the entire back wall. Sunlight shone through, softened by the peach colored, silky curtains. The laborers sat on colorful, plastic stools of various heights that loosely formed a messy circle of three rows. A few looked up curiously as we entered the room, but most continued on chatting with their neighbors without noticing us. Most of them seemed to be in their late twenties to early thirties, and two-thirds of the group were men. A small boy in black and yellow striped sweats acted out battle scenes with his action figures on the floor by the door.

Looking around, I realized that the people around me did not quite fit in the stereotype of "migrant laborers" I had in mind, built up from literary works and the media. They were not in ragged, old clothes full of patches, nor did they look depressed and stressed out. In fact, some of the women had dyed and permed their hair, resulting in light-brown, loose curls, and others had their hair styled

with decorative hair pieces. Their clothes looked similar to my own wardrobe, and I found myself admiring some of their jewelry. The men had a wider variety of clothes, from sandals and scrubs to leather-looking oxford shoes and button-up short sleeves. Some looked like they could be my teachers or my parents' coworkers.

After a deep breath, I squeezed past a couple of people, and placed myself in a corner in the back. My goal was to simply sit back and observe the crowd, as I wanted to learn how the service center conducted legal advice sessions and see how the migrant workers interacted with the consultants as well as with each other. I was pleasantly surprised to discover how easy it was for me to become invisible among the laborers. As soon as Xu called for people to quiet down and began her introductory speech, all gazes turned toward her. I fished out a notebook and pen from my bag, and studied the migrants around me, trying to take in as much as possible.

"In today's legal consulting session, we are going to learn about occupational injuries and deaths," announced Xu, as she scribbled gong shang on a large whiteboard as tall as she, "and the process of getting adequate compensation for such occurrences." The latter caused many to perk up, and a few around me shuffled in their seats excitedly. "Yeah!" shouted a deep voice, "Make them pay!" A few chimed in, "Dui, dui!" Some nervous giggles could be heard throughout the room. Xu's eyes twinkled, and she went on in a light-hearted manner, explaining the requirements needed for an injury to be counted as work-related. The workers listened intently. Some scribbled down notes on a piece of paper or notebook, some typed down the vital words on their smartphones. One man in front of me nodded enthusiastically to each of Xu's points, apparently having already known this information beforehand.

Next, Xu moved on to talk about the process of injury evaluations, explaining that there are ten levels - one being the most severe, and then the most minor. Depending on each workers' condition, the compensation may differ. Suddenly, a hand shot up in the air, and its owner yelled out with a strong southern accent: "Hey Director, what level do you think this would be?" Upon closer examination, it hit me that there were only three fingers - he was missing a pinky! Before I could catch my breath, a guy to my right stood up and waved around his left arm: "And this?!" There was a long, puckered ridge curling up across his forearm. While the wound was clearly months old, I could feel a stab of pain just from looking at it. Soon enough, everyone began showing their injured limbs, or

stumps where appendages used to be. I felt sick. I tried to take a deep breath, but the air was too muggy and dense. I missed the cool breeze of the AC. and I sat frozen to my stool, feeling numb. How did I miss these crucial details?

Right then, Xu's voice boomed through the sea of questions: "Alright everyone, honestly I don't know how you'd be rated; it's not up to me. But here at Southern Sparrow, we do have a chart that lists the requirements for each level. Make sure to grab a copy on your way out!" That managed to quiet most people down. However, someone else yelled from the back of the room: "Do minorities or younger people get more money?" I turned to see a hand raised up in the air; three of its fingers were only half the length of the index finger. It belonged to a young man in his late teens or early twenties. He popped his head above the sea of black hair to reveal a boyish grin: "The tip of these fingers were cut off, and it's difficult to scratch myself without nails!" The crowd laughed, and that seemed to stir up the group again. Some called for him to sit down in between giggles. "Go rub against the wall somewhere!" sounded a soft voice. "Or just find a wife to scratch for you!" belted another. "Any volunteers in this room?" joked yet another migrant.

"What's the rating for death?" wheezed an older man. The room instantly silenced as if we were sucked into a giant vacuum, and all heads turned to search for the source of that voice. "How much compensation," he paused to draw in a shallow breath, "is enough for a life?" His feeble delivery was barely a whisper, but the message thumped our hearts like a steel hammer. Through the roomful of people, I could make out a thin man who looked to be in his late thirties, dressed in a dark blue, short sleeved, cotton t-shirt that draped around his small figure, only outlining a hunched back. Underneath a similarly-colored-blue hat was a dark and wrinkled face. His expression was wary and weak, and his shoulders heaved up and down as he struggled with shortness of breath. This was a body already spent from a life-time of labor. I felt slightly suffocated just watching this shell of a body attempting to grasp the last remnants of life.

"This is Old Zhang," explained a Southern Sparrow volunteer who had been standing by the door, "his wife passed away last month of pneumoconiosis. Her factory refuses to pay for any of the treatment fees." The atmosphere was heavy; sighs could be heard across the room. Some shook their heads slowly. "Now he himself is in the second stage of the same illness." Here, she paused to look

over at him for confirmation, to which Zhang nodded solemnly before turning to look down at his feet. "In fact, that's his son over there," she continued, tilting her chin to point at the little boy I'd noticed earlier, "he's worried about what's going to happen to the child once his health worsens, but we are going to help him figure it out."

My mind wandered back to the readings I'd done on pneumoconiosis. So far, there hasn't been a cure, and the only medical treatments available are those that try to slow down the development. However, even such treatments are well beyond what migrant workers could afford, typically sending many families into extreme poverty and debt. Was this the case for this frail man before me? It was likely, but we never got a chance to learn his full story before Director Xu called for everyone to refocus. We needed to move on with the consulting lecture, so that people get all the necessary information before returning to work that very afternoon.

The next few hours went by quickly, as the director explained the steps of filing for compensation for occupational injuries, using clever delivery and effective examples. The audience continued to listen, occasionally interrupting with morbid jokes involving their own experiences. Several times, they chuckled collectively at the ridiculousness of the contradictions and inconsistencies presented by China's underdeveloped labor laws. Every now and then, there would be outcries of "What the hell is this?"—more out of despair than earnestly trying to figure it out. However, behind all the laughter and jests, were grave injuries, illnesses, and deaths. In the end, I stepped out of that conference room feeling exhausted and shaken.

Putting these faces to the statistics I had been reading about all summer was an extremely unsettling yet powerful experience. Those I had once tallied as figures have now become individuals, and in some cases, even friends. These people work 12 hour shifts to manufacture the products seen every day in our markets, clothing stores, tech shops, etc. Yet, often times in the face of glossy plastics or brightly colored fabrics, we as consumers give surprisingly little thought on the backstage politics along the supply chain. As China emerges as the world's factory, what becomes the cost behind each merchandise stamped with "Made in China?"

Book Review:
China Syndrome:
The True Story of the 21st Century 's first epidemic

Paul William Horak *graduated from Duke in May of 2013 and is currently living in Beijing, where he leads a research team at Peking University. His team is investigating Chinese hospital management practices in collaboration with academics from the US, UK and China. While at Duke he served as the President and later Editor-in-Chief at DEAN. He loves classic movies, good literature and the practice and pursuit of medicine. Next year he will start a post-bacc premedical program at Johns Hopkins University in Baltimore*

Karl Taro Greenfeld's China Syndrome is an fast-paced, fascinating, and easy to read account of the SARS epidemic that lacks a single argument, offering instead a succession of several thought-provoking points. Greenfeld, the Editor of TIME Asia when SARS struck, takes an expansive, largely character-driven approach in cataloging the spread of SARS from live-animal markets in Guandong - South East China - to Hong Kong, Beijing, Hanoi, Singapore, Taiwan, and eventually Toronto. For Greenfeld, the SARS saga is a humbling and cautionary tale. He shows that modern scientific research and medicine could do little to combat SARS beyond identifying its etiology. He also demonstrates the major political impediments to public health efforts to stave off the disease. These go far beyond local or national impediments: much of the book is devoted to the international battle between WHO officials in Geneva and Chinese leaders in Beijing. Greenfeld is very critical of the initial Chinese response to SARS and paints a damning portrait of a political regime that would sooner see its own people die than its grip on power threatened. If anything, Greenfeld's goal in writing China Syndome is to show how scientific, public health and political agendas often conflict with one another, and his argument is that this makes it hard to be truly prepared for an epidemic. That he does this through the lens of a host of compelling characters—one of which is the SARS virus, another the author himself—makes the work both very entertaining and very personal.

The book is divided into four parts that mirror the questions Chinese virologist Guan Yi asks when considering a virus. What is it? What does it do? Where does it come from? And how do you kill it? Throughout the pages of the book, which proceeds in strict chronological order and is at times overly dramatic and highly novelistic, the reader encounters the answers to three of these four questions. Even today, no one is quite sure about what "killed" SARS. There has not been a civilian SARS case since January 2004, with little, if any, research or publication on the disease since then. But we do have an idea of where it came from. Greenfeld's story starts in November 2002 with the odyssey of Fang Lin, a 24-year old migrant worker from a farming family in Jianxi, a largely agrarian province just north

of booming Guandong. Fang leaves Jiangxi and eventually finds work delivering and slaughtering live-animals for a Wild Flavor restaurant in Shenzhen, where patrons can sate their palate for wild civet cats and tropical snakes. Greenfeld suggests that it was in Wild Flavor markets and restaurants like the one that Fang worked in that the SARS virus made the species jump. Fang develops a cough, shortness of breath, fever and diarrhea and becomes too weak to work. He is too poor to consult a doctor and relies on traditional remedies or medicines bought from quack doctors to fight his illness.

While Fang Lin is fighting SARS, two virologists at the University of Hong Kong—Malik Peiris and Guan Yi—are busy hunting down avian flu. The deadly spread of an H5N1 strain in Penfold Park migratory birds in December of 2002 served as something of "red herring" in their search for SARS. Greenfeld noted how Peiris and Guan feared a repeat of the 1997 outbreak of H5N1 in Hong Kong leading them to obsess over finding the strain in samples taken from ailing patients in Guandong, and eventually Hong Kong. When both failed to find flu, they decided that they were likely up against a new viral agent. In the mean time, SARS was tearing through hospital emergency wards in Guandong and striking down health care workers with a vengeance. The disease, referred to as 'atypical pneumonia' by physicians and 'breath taker' (pp. 94-95) by the general population, made the move from Guandong to Hong Kong via afflicted nephrologist Liu Jianlun, who became a "superspreader of the disease " (p. 96). Staying on the Metropole Hotel's 9th floor, Liu infected 16 other guests, who would bring the SARS virus to Vietnam, Singapore, and Toronto. By this time 'atypical pneumonia' had already caught the attention of concerned health officials in Guandong. A team of doctors led by Zhong Nanshan, who would become one of the most celebrated physicians in China because of his effective response to SARS, had completed a report on the fatal nature of SARS and circulated it to the provincial leadership under Zhang Dejiang. The report, though accurate, was labeled neibu or "top secret" and consequently was not shared with the physicians fighting the epidemic (p. 90). Zhong Nanshan and Guan Yi, knowing the situation was dire, decided to defy government authority and collaborated to smuggle samples from Zhong's infected patients in Guandong to Guan's lab in Hong Kong. The epidemic had also reached China's capital, the stronghold of the Chinese Communist Party, Beijing.

It is at this juncture in the story that Greenfeld highlights the conflicting agendas of WHO officials in Geneva and Chinese leaders in Beijing. China's leaders were in a bit of a bind: Paramount leader Jiang Zemin was scheduled to install Hu Jintao as his successor less than two weeks (3/15/03) after the first cases of SARS were reported in Beijing hospitals (3/3/03). Moreover, because most cases were being treated in military hospitals—which would be under Jiang's jurisdiction even after the formal transfer of power—there was at least some cause for confusion among Beijing's ruling elite. Should they be loyal to Hu or Jiang? WHO officials had arrived in Beijing in late February but were not granted an audience with Chinese public health officials for weeks. They were also denied access to Guandong, the "ground zero" for SARS. It soon became evident to Greenfeld—alone in panic stricken Hong Kong—that the government must be covering things up. Three days after Hu Jintao was named the President of China, Peiris and colleagues at the University of Hong Kong announced the discovery of the pathogen responsible SARS—a coronavirus. Three weeks later, on 4/8/03, TIME's Susan Jakes published a groundbreaking story on the whistleblower Jiang Yanyong, a high-ranking party member and semi-retired surgeon, who confirmed that the SARS epidemic in Beijing was far worse than official numbers suggested.

The TIME story, according to Greenfeld, was a bombshell. It not only resulted in the eventual ousting of Beijing Mayor, Meng Xuenong, and Chinese Minister of Health, Zhang Wenkang, but also made SARS impossible to ignore. Hu Jintao, in a bold political move, staked his leadership on the effective containment and eradication of SARS. The eventual success of his campaign helped him to consolidate power and distance himself from his predecessor Jiang Zemin. Here Greenfeld muses about the efficacy of China's dictatorship in first suppressing news on SARS and then containing it. He also credits the WHO's foresight and heroism in leading the global campaign to first find the SARS virus and later identify, isolate and treat suspected SARS cases. But he remains skeptical as to how responsible Chinese and WHO efforts were in actually bringing about the disappearance of the disease. Did we just get lucky?

Greenfeld gives a comprehensive and balanced account of the Chinese experience with SARS, but it is not without its limitations. Although the book does an excellent job of stitching together the stories of a number of different dramatis personae, it fails to put

one of its most important into context—namely the SARS virus. Greenfeld often compares SARS to H5N1, Ebola and other recent infectious diseases but he devotes little time to discussing these afflictions and how they have challenged scientists and pubic health officials. This is done in Thomas Abraham's Twenty-First Century Plague: the story of SARS, and would add to Greenfeld's already impressive treatment of virology in China Syndrome. (See reviews on Abraham's book below.) This is the only major limitation of Greenfeld's book, which is on the whole balanced and comprehensive. Unlike Abraham, Greenfeld tells the stories of people living with SARS outside of Mainland China and Hong Kong, devoting a series of chapters to the initial outbreaks in Hanoi, Singapore and Toronto. He also captures the stress and panic associated with living through such a frightening epidemic from a number of different vantage points: doctors, nurses, scientists, government officials, family members of SARS patients, and even survivors of SARS. Greenfeld's novelistic writing places the reader in the lonely hotel rooms, sterile labs and crowded hospital wards where SARS was experienced.

One of the main criticisms of Greenfeld's writing is that it expresses a strong anti-China bias. In his review of China Syndrome, Frederic Keck writes that "all of the complex interaction between the Chinese government and the local elite escapes Greenfeld, who remains attached to a fixed, monolithic and ultimately very negative image of China." This is unfair and untrue. One of the highlights of Greenfeld's narrative is his assessment of China's initial non-response to SARS. He understands the complexity of China's political machine, the frailty of China's Communist Party, and the history of its manipulation of the Chinese public—and is frustrated by them. This is hardly a rare or surprising view, especially in light of the contents of China Syndrome. While it is fair to say that Greenfeld has a negative view of the Chinese government, probably borne from his background in journalism (where all authority is questioned), it is not fair to say that he has a negative image of China. In fact, the first 30 pages of the book are a testament to Greenfeld's interest in the lives of contemporary everyday Chinese. Throughout the book he travels to the rural countryside and urban slums to trace the movement of SARS. His point in these chapters is not to highlight how dirty or backwards parts of China might be, but instead to highlight how vulnerable they are. He forwards a rather uncontroversial view (even to Chinese): that China's high growth has come at the expense of the

country's environmental and public health. Guandong in 2003 had the perfect storm of factors contributing to the origin and spread of SARS. "Epidemics reveal the strengths and weaknesses of the societies in which they occur." (MacDougall)

This is not a new view by any stretch of the imagination. In fact, we encountered very similar reasoning in Charles Rosenberg's The Cholera Years, when he catalogued New York City's experiences with cholera in 1832, 1849 and 1866. It was a "great time to be a germ" in 1849 New York: sanitation had not kept up with rapid urbanization and the city was a dirty, overcrowded, mess. Rosenberg makes constant reference to the garbage-littered streets and domestic animals, mainly pigs, which served as the city's only waste management force. In short, NYC in 1849 had the perfect storm of factors contributing to the origin and spread of cholera. In Margaret Humphreys's Yellow Fever and the South, we see that late 19th century New Orleans had a similar predisposition to yellow fever outbreaks because of its function as a trading port with the tropics, where the disease was endemic, and its location below sea level, which necessitated the use of cisterns, which provided mosquito larvae with a place to develop. It took New York and New Orleans decades to mount the appropriate public health responses. The eradication of cholera was aided by John Snow's observations of drinking water in 1850's London, but vibrio cholera was not widely known until Robert Koch isolated it in 1884. The aedes egypti mosquito was not accepted as the vector of yellow fever until 1901, after experiments done by Walter Reed in Cuba. Public health efforts aimed at prevention were ultimately what conquered cholera and yellow fever in the United States. That the SARS virus first appeared in November 2002, did not become public until February 2003, and was ultimately isolated by Peiris just a month later is indeed an impressive scientific achievement. In the span of 100 hundred years, scientific research has gone from taking years, even decades, to isolate a disease to mere months.

But prevention and control are another matter. Greenfeld makes the point that Chinese prevention and control of SARS were handicapped by politics. Chinese government officials new that a terrible disease was making the rounds of hospital wards in Guandong and Beijing, but decided to cover it up for the sake of preserving stability at a time of great uncertainty, given the leadership transition. By withholding knowledge, outlawing coordination, and keeping WHO officials out of affected regions, the Chinese government put healthcare workers at greater risk

and increased the probability of SARS spreading from one locale to the next. There were some instances where doctors like Zhong Nanshan and Jiang Yanyang defied orders, but the majority of people did nothing. When one of Greenfeld's field reporters asked a Beijing doctor, "How could you do this?" his response was only, "We are ashamed (p. 337) ." Eventually, the empire struck back at SARS—with Hu Jintao leading a countrywide effort to prevent and contain the disease. Within days, fever detectors, were set up across the country and safety precautions were being broadcast to all in earshot of a TV or radio.

On the other side of the world, in SARS-struck Toronto, Sheela Basrur the city's Minister of Health, had far fewer resources and much less authority with which to strike back. Her organization, Toronto Public Health, was unprepared and underequipped due to chronic underfunding. She also had to contend with a lack of coordination between federal, provincial and city organizations. Ironically, Toronto was halfway through the creation of a provincial pandemic response guideline when SARS arrived—it would have to wing its response to the disease. Eventually, SARS disappeared from Chinese and Canadian hospitals. Both mounted successful public health responses to the SARS epidemic, but would the responses have been effective in combating a more contagious disease like the flu of 1918? Politics in both countries had contributed to a less than robust public health response. In China, government leaders initially covered up the epidemic, perhaps enabling its spread to places as far away as Canada. In Toronto, politicians decided not to fully fund the public health department, which may have been partially responsible for a lack of resources and coordination when SARS arrived. As we have seen time and again throughout the semester, the first response to an epidemic is often denial. Denial allows business to continue unimpeded, and it prevents the panics that disrupt civil society. But it also costs lives, as the SARS case made apparent. Public health responses to epidemics seem to always be "too late" because they are often mounted only when things become to bad to ignore or deny.

Greenfeld's China Syndrome lends modern day context to many of the fundamental questions that our class has sought to answer through looking at history. Who is responsible for public health? What diseases are acted on? How do science and politics interact to promote or inhibit public health? China's, indeed the world's, experience with SARS shows just how complicated some of these answers can be. In 2003, China was the engine for the world's

economic growth (it still is) and was more connected to the global movement of people and goods than at any point in its long history. In theory, SARS was a 15-hour flight away from Washington, DC. A 12-hour flight away from Geneva. A 4-hour flight away from Tokyo. We should care about public health in China. As Greenfeld makes clear in his chapters based in Hanoi, Toronto and Singapore—China's negligence cost lives abroad. Globalization makes us all vulnerable. But still China refused help from the WHO, and refused to let WHO officials into affected regions. Is this behavior likely to be unique to China? Greenfeld points out how the SARS epidemic simultaneously showed just how essential the WHO was in monitoring and preventing disease outbreaks, and just how limited also. The irony is that public health is a truly global challenge that remains bounded by national concerns. This is not all that different from cholera and yellow fever outbreaks in the 19th century. The biggest difference is that we now have the tools to understand disease—whether or not those tools help us to combat and contain disease is another question. I always wondered why SARS, which claimed just 774 lives—so small a number, especially when a country of 1.3 billion people is involved—was such a big deal. Greenfeld's book offers a compelling answer: the coordination, communication and capacity needed to effectively deal with epidemics like the one sparked by SARS are not as sophisticated as we are often led to believe.

Works Cited

Book Reviews:[1]

http://www.nejm.org/doi/full/10.1056/NEJM200508043530523

http://chinaperspectives.revues.org/2763

http://www.ncbi.nlm.nih.gov/pmc/articles/PMC1421373/

Books:

Abraham, Thomas. Twenty-first Century Plague: The Story of SARS. Baltimore, MD: Johns Hopkins UP, 2005. Print.

Greenfeld, Karl Taro. China Syndrome: The True Story of the 21st Century's First Great Epidemic. New York, NY: HarperCollins, 2006. Print.

Humphreys, Margaret. Yellow Fever and the South. New Brunswick: Rutgers UP, 1992. Print.

Rosenberg, Charles E. The Cholera Years. Chicago: University of Chicago, 1987. Print.

Articles:

Toronto's Health Department in Action: Influenza in 1918 and SARS in 2003 (Sakai)

http://www.nytimes.com/2005/05/15/health/15sars.html?_r=0

---

[*]There was only one appropriate book review for China Syndrome, so I decided to read reviews of Abraham's Twenty-first Century Plague and integrate a brief comparison between the two works in my own review. They seem to be quite complementary.

Paul William
Horak

www.ingramcontent.com/pod-product-compliance
Lightning Source LLC
Chambersburg PA
CBHW080947290526
45795CB00009B/2939